Eat Good Things
Every Day

First published in 2009 by Atrium
Atrium is an imprint of Cork University Press
Youngline Industrial Estate, Pouladuff Road, Togher, Cork, Ireland

British Library Cataloguing in Publication Data

A CIP catalogue record for this book is available from the British Library.

ISBN 978-0955226-13-7

Book design and typesetting, Anú Design, Tara
Printed in Navarra, Spain, by Graphy Cems Ltd

For all Atrium books visit www.corkuniversitypress.com

Eat Good Things Every Day

Bringing good food to the family table

CARMEL SOMERS

63

226

128

74

Contents

195

147

283

174

In loving memory of

Bob and Debbie

with whom we shared many

happy family meals

Foreword

Good Things Café is sited at the western end of the village of Durrus in west Cork. Its stunning view across Dunmanus Bay and easy access to the sea bring through its doors not just the customers impatient for Carmel Somers' 'Plates' of the day, but also the local producers, hunters and gatherers who swing with familiar ease through the glass door bringing them straight into the restaurant and kitchen, where they are rewarded with Carmel's infectious smile as they haul in their bounty for her loving inspection. It could be the lady who scours the beaches for the seaweed used in some of the dishes – only last week on a two-day course the students were baking scones with the dulse she had just harvested – or it could be the fisherman still in his waders carrying his bucket of scallops alive in their shells. Every one of the artisans who enter the portals of Good Things Café is involved in some way or another with locally grown, harvested or handmade food. No wonder the kitchen is a place of wonder and curiosity where the Slow Food ideal has been totally embraced.

Cauldrons of steaming fish, vegetable and chicken stock simmer away on the huge gas burners at the back of the kitchen like gigantic sentinels overlooking the rest of the food preparation. We have come a long way from the drab post-war food I was brought up to expect. Little surprise then that, after my first visit to Paris aged 15, I was a willing convert to an entirely new way of life.

Breakfast in the tiny French apartment: a baguette bought minutes earlier from the bakery downstairs and a bowl of steaming hot chocolate. We were even encouraged to dip the warm crusty slice into the thick chocolaty mixture. I was hooked. Much later, during the 1980s, a similar experience would alter for ever the young student Carmel. Paris was where she 'worked her socks off' in a restaurant called Lous Landes, but this was also where her own 'great awakening' occurred. She saw at first hand the way in which the French, with reverential respect, enjoyed the talking and the eating of their food. Mealtimes were a time to catch up, to listen and learn, to discuss the dishes and to offer a running critique on the manner in which they had been prepared without the cook in any way getting upset at the feedback. This is where our young student learned not only how to 'balance' a meal but also the subtlety of adding a salad and a pudding or fruit that would best round things off.

As inspiration I had Miss Whitty, my domestic science teacher, and a wonderful cook called Arabella Boxer, who invited a very young me to her home one evening for dinner and gave me my first gull's egg to taste. Carmel's equivalent was Madame de Villeneuve, who taught her the self-same principles of cooking that would be the foundation stone of Good Things Café. How for instance taking vegetables from the garden and pouring tap water and the proper seasoning at the right moment, and with a dash of patience, could produce an amazing soup. Add some homemade crusty bread, light a candle and, hey presto. A feast! Carmel also gives Madame de Villeneuve the credit for proving to her how, without a shred of fuss and with just four ingredients easily available in Ireland, like beef and carrots, you could create a really superb dinner or a soufflé from yesterday's leftovers in the fridge. Carmel, who loved her entire French experience, was finally hooked herself; she would never look back. She literally fell in love.

What first attracted me to Carmel's spirit and ethos of living, cooking and teaching during the summer of 2005, when David and I would often pop by for lunch, was in part the deep-rooted affection she holds for other chefs and cooks. Elizabeth David, Jane Grigson, Stephen Bull and obituaries of the great and the good, with whom Carmel feels a particular bond, stare out at us from her walls as a reminder that food is an ever-changing process. The ingredients may stay the same but it is the artistry with those ingredients, the alchemy, that is forever altering like great design in fashion and architecture. Our experiences have become more finely honed with travel, allowing us to discover new tastes and try out new ideas. Surely this is one of the things that keeps the creative process truly alive. Generations of masters of the kitchen have left us a wealth of knowledge in books and more recently on television; they not only cajole and inspire us, but our debt to them requires that we take firm hold of the baton passed to us with a pledge to pass it on to the next generation. This is what Carmel does at the Good Things School. She is not just a great cook, she is a vibrant and generous teacher who, like all great educationalists, wants us to be captivated by the joy of food that has infused her life. You might be forgiven, at first glance, for thinking that Good Things Café is in fact a library which also happens to serve food. The books she loves, and which have most influenced her, are stacked high on every available shelf for us all to dip into and get similarly 'hooked'. So are her favourite products of the moment, be it olive oil, wine, flour, vinegar, oats, salt and a whole host of other enticing groceries. So in the end it all comes down to this: when you enter the Good Things Café you are entering Carmel's world. She displays, like the consummate artist she is, all the things past and present that have contributed to the building of her universe, which happily for those of us living in west Cork, she is prepared to share.

Patsy Puttnam, 8 February 2009

Acknowledgements

There are a number of people who I would like to thank for bringing this book to fruition. The book would never have happened if Mike Collins of Cork University Press had not approached me to write it, and if he had not then had endless patience with me. I would also like to thank Maria O'Donovan, my editor, whose happy voice cheered me up as she kept the project going. Thanks too to Karen Carty of Anú Design for her design; Gloria Greenwood for all her time; and everybody else at Cork University Press.

A big thank you to all the staff, past and present, at Good Things especially Rebeca, Christina, Fiona and Joy for all their hard work and dedication. Thank you to Ita Sweeney, Freddie O'Mahoney and Marie Murphy for everything. And a special thank you to John Carey for amazing photography; he was a joy to work with.

The biggest thank you of all goes to my three girls, who for two years supported me in every way. Ellen and Jill helped with the recipes, eating everything I cooked, giving their honest opinion and patiently asking 'are you finished the book yet?' Briony gave endless help with the writing and testing of the recipes, making the Good Things plan work, and taking charge of the store cupboard and shopping lists.

I would like to thank all who have taught me over the years: Sister Benedict OSB; the De Montault family; Colin White for six wonderful years of cooking by his side; and Stephen Markwich for sharing so much with me. Thank you to all our lovely customers at Good Things who come back year after year and keep asking for the book.

A special thank you goes to Patsy and David Puttnam for all their help and support. Thanks also to Susan Boland and Anne Keogh who encouraged the book concept, and Mary Keane for sharing recipes and ideas.

I would also like to send a big thank you to everbody who very patiently answered me when I asked 'what are you cooking for supper tonight?' Finally, thank you to my brother John and his wife Camilla, without whose encouragement Good Things would not have started.

Introduction

One Saturday evening last winter I went to my local supermarket to pick up the last few things that were on my shopping list. As I went to get a basket I met Maria with two of her children. She said, 'I wish I could follow you and see what you are buying. I just don't know where to start', as she piled vegetables into her trolley. 'You don't have a list?' I replied. She gave me a puzzled look and we parted. As a mother of three children I could empathise with her. When I was at the checkout packing my bag I could see her on the second aisle and thought, will she use every-thing that is in her trolley and will she have to make a return visit during the week. Maria had attended many of my cookery classes, had lots of my recipes and shelves of cookbooks and yet preparing meals seemed such a chore, especially with a young family. As I headed to collect my order from the fish shop I realised that people did not know how to plan their meals, shop efficiently and buy just what they needed.

As one who runs a restaurant and cookery school, I know that planning and list-making are the tools of the trade. They are second nature to me now. It struck me that these basic skills, which I also apply at home, would therefore help anyone who has to cook. As a mother working at home or in the restaurant, I feel my day flows better when I have planned the main meal.

During one of my cookery classes, one of the students was not very relaxed, so, over lunch, I asked her if she was enjoying the class. I was delighted with her honesty when she replied that she didn't enjoy cooking anymore; it was hard work, she had no new ideas and felt even more lost when she opened her many cookbooks. Thinking of our conversation and also of Maria in the supermarket, I could see a need for a cookbook on our shelves – a book that would give dishes for a couple of months with a weekly shopping list, bearing in mind that all ingredients need to be readily available. Strolling through the markets, seeing what is available and being inspired by fresh seasonal produce can be very enjoyable but is a lifestyle only suited to those of us who lead food-orientated lives. In this situation one buys, then goes home and decides what dish can be created. This is the total reverse of the objective of my book, which is to plan, buy and cook.

Anyone can learn to cook. All one needs is a cookbook, a few utensils and a basic cooker. However, the purpose of this book is to show people who have huge demands on their time how manageable good home-cooking can be. Planning is the initial challenge; cooking is the easy part. Once you get into the habit of planning, cooking will be a more relaxed affair.

In preparing this book my dream is to show people how easy it is to cook, eat well and enjoy the whole experience – I hope it works.

Getting Started

A few points to remember about cooking.

- Relax – a happy cook cooks well.
- Recipes are guidelines and ideas.
- Taste, touch and smell as you cook. You will develop your own taste.
- Don't rush.
- Remember you are not a chef so don't try recreating restaurant food.
- You cannot please everybody. So cook to satisfy your palate. This always gives the best results, as you will adjust as you cook.
- Give yourself as much worktop space as is possible. Clear away all bits and pieces you do not need.
- Tidy up as you go – but not obsessively.
- If something goes wrong, try again. Lots of mistakes are edible. New dishes are often created by mistakes.
- If you don't know, ask.
- Always set the table, even for the simplest of meals.
- When cooking for friends, keep it simple. Always cook something in advance; you should not spend the evening in the kitchen. Don't invite people that you feel you have to impress. Cook a dish you have cooked before.
- If you cook, someone else should wash up!
- The biggest treat is to have dinner cooked for you.

Feeding Children

Feeding children is the same as feeding adults. I never understand why there should be a difference and often wonder when this started. Who decided what was children's food? What is marketed as children's food very often is processed packaged food, low in nutrition and high in preservatives. Such food provides a very poor diet and is very expensive. The problem is that children get used to the taste of so-called "kids food" and never develop a taste for pure fresh food. Don't start cooking separate meals for adults and children. All children go through fads and phases. If they don't become an issue, most of these are short-lived. An hour or two of playing outside, a walk or a swim can get children eating just about anything. When they know there is no choice, they won't expect it. Children love strong tastes (salty crisps, sour sweets) and if a child can eat a sweet called "toxic waste" I am sure they could be encouraged to try an olive. They love trying new things and being involved in the cooking and preparing of the meal, including setting the table, especially if there is a candle to light! I have noticed that when my children cook a dish (with or without my help), they are very proud of it, like to eat it and will make sure it gets eaten.

Bribery is a very important ingredient in getting children to try new foods and to finish what's on their plate. A tub of ice-cream is a great stand-by and occasionally the promise of a square of chocolate can work wonders.

Encourage children to drink water. Fizzy drinks should be a very rare treat.

Do not waste food

Try not to throw out any food.

Every week I find there is something else I can avoid wasting by popping it in the freezer.

Double cream can be frozen and used at a later date to make a gratin, soup (see chowder recipe page 258) or in mashed potatoes (see page 35).

All types of cheese can be frozen and used to top pizzas and bakes or mixed into a pasta dish. This is worth remembering – especially after Christmas, when we all buy too much cheese.

When you have an abundance of herbs such as parsley, coriander, basil or a mixture just purée them to a fine paste with a little olive oil. Store in a container topped with oil and it will keep in the fridge for weeks.

Make a soup or stew with bits left over in the fridge. Last weekend I made a stew-like soup from the fridge.
I had about:
1 pint of chicken stock
½ pint of tomato sauce
6 cooked potatoes
A piece of ginger, which I grated
1 bunch of spinach, chopped
I put everything together in a saucepan except the potatoes and spinach and brought it to the boil, then added a handful of puy lentils and simmered it for 20 minutes. Finally I added the potatoes and spinach and simmered for five minutes. I ended up with four big bowls of warming tasty soup for lunch, with mimimal effort and an empty fridge.

Equipment

We all have too much clutter in our kitchens but still we seem to be missing some of the basics. When cooking the dishes for the book I realised how few pieces of equipment I really needed. When we put them together to take a picture I was more surprised with what we had never used. I had six wooden spoons and only needed one, two colanders (two cool colours!) and only needed one, two extra saucepans but one was red and heart-shaped and I had to buy it!!

Yes, I have the trendy kitchen aid and the magimix but I don't use them every day. When cooking for small numbers, chopping and mixing can be done by hand.

Nearly all kitchen equipment should last you nearly a lifetime. I have had my knives, peppermill and two of my saucepans for 25 years and hope to have them for another 25.

Good quality does not always mean expensive. You will be surprised where you will find some bits and pieces. I bought two medium-sized frying pans years ago in a corner shop for £10 and they are still in use. Apart from frying, I use them for pies, gratins and bakes. Look for saucepans, frying pans and oven trays that are heavy-based and suitable for hob and oven. If you get the opportunity to buy standard catering equipment, do avail of it. They may not look too trendy but what they lack in looks they certainly compensate for in durability and functionality.

At home I only ever use a chopping knife and a small vegetable knife. I buy my fish filleted or whole depending on how I plan on cooking it. The same applies to meat, so I never need filleting or boning knives.

I use a serrated knife (bread knife) to cut tomatoes and segment oranges.

A zester is very useful for taking the zest from citrus fruit. I find I lose so much with a grater.

Heat diffusers are perfect for keeping a low heat.

An ovenproof plate is ideal for finishing a roast chicken or meat while you make gravy.

Roasting trays should be shallow, no more that 3–4cm (and heavy-based), thus ensuring the meat will roast perfectly. I often roast in a frying pan; the handle helps for getting it in and out of the oven.

An oven tray for roasting vegetables and potatoes should have very low sides, about 1–2cm. This helps the vegetables to roast quickly and avoids stewing. I find the grill tray good for this.

A meat or fish slice with a short handle gives you more control.

Wok – buy a cheap, thin, lightweight wok. This heats quickly and reduces the risk of stewing, allowing you to stirfry. I bought mine for a tenner.

A vegetable mouli is best for perfect mashed potatoes and is also very handy for making soups and fruit purées.

Avoid glass and marble chopping boards. They ruin your knife and make a horrible noise. Remember to put a damp cloth under your board when using.

Keep plastic containers with lids for storing food in the fridge and freezer. Also milk and cream cartons are ideal for freezing stocks and soups.

Oven – get to know your oven. Don't always trust the temperature; test it and work from there. Oven temperatures in recipes are a guide.

Microwaves – should be banned, as they ruin food!

Spice grinder – I have a separate coffee grinder to grind spices, as I like to buy whole spices. Cumin-flavoured coffee does not work!

Notes on Ingredients
Used in the Book

Nearly all the ingredients used in the recipes should be easy to get from most supermarkets and health food shops. If there is something they don't have, most are happy to get it for you. Our local shop here in Durrus stocks some amazing ingredients – fresh chillies, ginger, organic yoghurts, proper bacon, unrefined sugar and much more. If the owners take pride in what they do, they are always happy to help

Apple juice – lots of freshly pressed juice is available. The good stuff always seems to come in bottles. If you drive through Waterford, Wexford or Tipperary you can easily pick some up. At the café we use a lovely juice from Con Trass in Clonmel. We serve it as an alternative to wine and use it in a lot of dishes.

Pesto – when buying pesto, check the ingredients. It should be made with olive oil and pinenuts, not sunflower and peanuts. Don't presume organic means the right ingredients. If you ever manage to get a couple of bunches of basil, do make your own. It will keep, covered with oil, in the fridge for weeks.

Chillies – if they are not easy to get, use dried: soak them in boiling water for 15 minutes to soften and remember they are always a little hotter than fresh. I use a lot of chillies; they are a powerful antioxidant, contain vitamin C and iron and can become addictive. Always add chillies to suit your taste.

Ginger – I use a lot. It's always in the shops and really cheers food up and warms us from the inside. When buying ginger it should feel firm, otherwise it is old and will be woody inside. If you have some left in your fridge, don't throw it out, grate and freeze it.

Frozen food – peas, spinach, runner beans and raspberries freeze well and can have many uses. These fill the gaps now and again.

Nuts – buy in small amounts; they don't keep well.

Spices – buy in small quantites; health food shops, markets and trips abroad are the best source. Store in light-proof containers, as light fades the colour and flavour. I store mine in an unfashionable lunch box. Spices have many health benefits.

Saffron – make sure it is from Spain or Kashmir. Yes it is expensive, but a little goes a long way and is a lovely addition to a dish. Remember not to use too much, as the flavour is strong and too much is unpleasant. Do count the strands; if a recipe says six only use six, providing it is the best quality.

Vanilla – you cannot beat the pods, they are well worth the money. After use wash, dry and store them with sugar for a few weeks and you will have your own vanilla sugar – great on porridge.

Salt – buy good sea salt for cooking and a box of Maldon salt for salads. Now you can get sea salt mixed with seaweed, which I love when cooking fish and is also lovely on roast lamb.

Smoked haddock – most smoked haddock that is available is dyed. Look for undyed smoked haddock, which is naturally smoked and is delicious eaten raw with a squeeze of lemon juice.

Butter – I use very little butter in cooking but when I use it it has to be the real thing. Butter tastes pure. Margarine tastes horrible and the flavour is never masked in cooking.

Olive oil – we are now so snobbish about olive oil. Try and buy something you like the tase of. Be guided by the flavour and don't be fooled by a fancy bottle; I have.

Chowder mix – don't buy it. Buy a piece of fish and cut it up.

Pears – always buy a week before you need them and leave them out of the fridge to ripen.

Soy sauce, Tamari – is wheat free.

Sugar – I like the unrefined sugars and now only buy the regular and a soft brown. I once had five different sugars in my cupboard, some with just a spoon taken out. I never use castor sugar.

Garlic – should feel firm. Buy Spanish garlic, if available. A lot of the shops sell Chinese garlic, which has been in cold storage for a very long time and lacks flavour and ends up sprouting after a few days in your kitchen. Health food shops very often sell very good quality garlic.

Dried sour cherries – not always easy to get. Can be found in most health food shops. Lovely to eat from the packet. Great with yoghurt for breakfast. Also lovely with lamb (see page 229).

Fish – usually better from a fish shop or a market stall. Get to know your fishmonger. Fish should not smell, should have nice shiny skin and whole fish should have clear eyes. I like shops and stalls that don't have too much choice. Ask the fishmonger to fillet, skin and scale fish for you if required. Try to buy locally caught fish.

Meat – try to buy from a butcher, as usually the meat is hung longer. Beef should be hung for up to three weeks. Well-hung beef will cost a little more but will be better value, as it will be very tender to eat. **Chickens** are not cheap if they are reared well. Whole chickens are better value than portions, especially fillets, and you have the carcass for a stock.

Pork – buy from a butcher that kills his own. Most butchers sell good beef and lamb, but only some do good pork and chicken. I like butchers that mostly cut the meat to order. Get to know your butcher and ask about their meat. They should be proud of what they are selling and happy to help.

Rice – my favourite is organic short grain brown rice. I started using it years ago after I read Denis Cotter's *The Café Paradiso Cookbook*. In the chapter on rice he explains "because of the amount of chemicals used in the production of rice it is not a good idea to eat wholegrain rice unless it is certified organic. The husk [which is on brown rice] diligently holds almost all the residual poisons." Brown rice cooked as it is in the recipe on page 29 will taste nutty and have a lovely texture. As a family we eat at least a kilo a week. Having it in the fridge, cooked, makes for a quick snack at any time of the day.

Organic – I buy most of my store-cupboard items organic: flour, sugars, dried fruit, nuts, lentils and oats. Most of them don't cost much more and are worth it, for the taste alone. Some super-markets carry a wide range of organic produce. I find usually the health food shops carry a wider range and offer a personal service.

Bacon – not always what it says on the packet. As Jane Grigson wrote in 1978 in her *Vegetable Book*, "you might think that all smoked bacon is smoked, all green bacon unsmoked. Things, though, are not always what they seem: 'smoked' these days can mean 'flavoured approximately with chemicals'. The difference is obvious once you become familiar with the real, right thing. You soon realise which hams and bacons have been painted and injected to simulate cured meat." I find when I buy bacon or ham from producers like Gubbeen, near me here in West Cork, I don't need to soak it as it has been cured in a brine and not with excess salt.

Use-by dates – don't always trust them. Some things last longer than the date (e.g. cream, yoghurt, jams and chutney). A couple of extra days are taken off fresh produce to cover car travel and bad storage. Always smell or taste. At the moment I am eating jam that is one year out of date. Don't waste food.

If your local shop/supermarket does not stock something you need, do let them know. They will only carry an item if there is demand for it.

Herbs

Adding herbs to cooking does make a difference to the flavour. They add that something extra to a dish. They can make something plain come to life. The problem is we don't always have access to fresh herbs. If I cannot get fresh herbs, I go without. With the odd exception, such as oregano in the right dishes and cooked into the food.

I will go without herbs if the only choice I have is the overpriced offerings sold in the supermarket – is the plastic more expensive than what they carry? My solution is to have a pot of rosemary, thyme, bay (dry the leaves before use, which will take about a week in a warm kitchen) and parsley outside the door. These are all easy to get and don't need much looking after.

I divide herbs in two, hard and soft. Hard herbs are usually the woody kind such as rosemary, thyme and bay, which take a lot of cooking. Soft herbs are the more delicate ones like chives, basil, coriander and dill. Parsley I find fits between both and works with nearly everything, it is such a good herb, easy to grow, easy to buy all year round and so easy to use.

Curly or flat-leaf parsley? I don't mind as long as they are fresh. Curly is easier to grow. Flat-leaf parsley has become trendy.

Remember to chop the stalks of any soft herbs and add them to the dish at the start of cooking.

Getting the Good Things Plan

Meals for Monday to Friday are deliberately kept simple. Nobody wants to spend a lot of time in the kitchen after a long day at work. I love to cook but it does become a chore when you have to produce a meal every day of the year. Try to come up with something different, healthy, balanced, but at the same time taking into account family likes and dislikes. I have divided the recipes into two sections: four weeks using winter ingredients (1–4) and four using what is more readily available in the summer (5–8). These are mostly interchangeable, with the odd exception, such as mackerel and rhubarb (summer and winter respectively). Even though I have divided the weeks into winter and summer, they will work well if you run them together. I have also included eight soups and eight easy desserts at the back of the book. Some of the soups you will be able to make with ingredients you have left over in the fridge at the end of the week.

The first chapter is one on basics, covering everything from bread to gravy to stocks. During the weeks you will refer back to this chapter for preparations needed to make your week easier. The following eight chapters each detail cooking for a full week.

Starting on a Saturday (or your own chosen day), you will need to do your shopping and preparation for the week ahead. Saturday evening is a fish dish that is quick to prepare after all the shopping. Sunday is roast with a little extra for another meal during the week. Monday is another fish night using the fish purchased earlier in the week. Tuesday and Wednesday are quick meals, one vegetarian, another using up leftovers from Sunday. Thursday we have another quick simple midweek dish, with some extra time to prepare a one-pot meal which can be reheated on Friday evening. This way we feel that we have an evening off from the kitchen when we can relax, catch up with family and have a lovely meal with not a takeaway in sight!

to Work for You

The store cupboard list which follows has been drawn up with the hope of providing you with all the non-perishables needed for the entire eight weeks. This includes some large quantities, for example 14 tins of tomatoes, the idea being that, if these bulky items are bought together in one go, weekly shopping will be lighter, easier and more efficient. Also calculated are the precise amounts needed for many of the smaller store-cupboard components such as pinenuts (120g) and prunes (750g). If the closest to the necessary amount is bought, you will avoid overloading your kitchen with excessive amounts of ingredients which may be hard to use.

The shopping lists have been formulated with a similar aim. You will notice certain meats are only purchased if you do not have the leftovers from a previous recipe. Butter, for instance, is not used a great amount in my cooking but is present in some recipes. I have reasoned that you therefore will only need to buy butter in weeks one and five. I have tried to consider all elements for these lists, but the best way to ensure you do not over-buy or waste food is to check the list against your fridge before you leave home.

I have chosen potatoes, rice or couscous to go with each meal, but these can be changed to suit your taste or whatever you have in your cupboard.

There are only two pasta recipes in the book. Everybody knows how to cook pasta. It is quick and simple but we are eating too much of it. Children love pasta and I know some children would eat it five nights of the week. I always have pasta in the cupboard as I like to use it with leftovers (see meat sauce, page 127). When I have leftover roast vegetables that include roast garlic and tomatoes, I whizz them up and serve them with pasta, adding some toasted pinenuts and cheese. Sometimes I fry some breadcrumbs mixed with garlic and chopped almonds, toast them in a pan with some olive oil until crisp and toss into the pasta with some leftover cooked green vegetables such as broccoli.

I am not a vegetarian, but at least once a week I like to prepare a complete vegetarian meal while other nights I might not bother cooking a vegetable to complement my meat or fish dish, being quite happy with potatoes or rice and a green salad.

We always eat fruit after dinner and I would only make a dessert as a treat or when I am having friends around. I find winter time is when I long for a comfort pudding, hot from the oven, and our family favourite is the rice pudding on page 283.

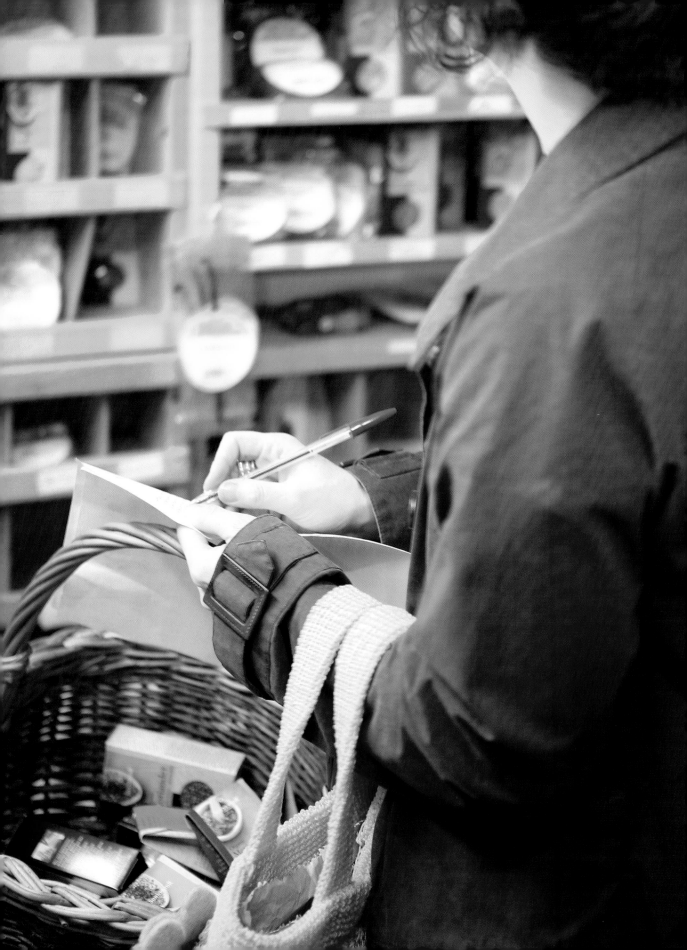

Food Shopping

Food shopping can become a chore week in week out. Most of us have to do it. Here are a few ideas to make it easier. Lists are the way to go. I live by lists in the restaurant and at home. Buying food and then planning your dishes can lead to more trips to the shops and a lot of waste. Try to do your week's shopping in one trip.

1. Make a list of the dishes you want to cook for the week ahead.
2. Make a list of ingredients needed for the recipes.
3. Check your list off with your fridge and store cupboard, crossing off anything you already have. You will not remember when you get to the shop.
4. Make your list out under headings (see shopping lists in book).
5. Phone orders through to fish shop and butcher. Even our local health food shop takes phone orders.
6. If you can pick up fish during the week while at work, write a note in your diary.

7.   There are now many good local markets. If you are lucky enough to have one in your town then approach it with your shopping list – your list is most important here. With all my experience I still yield to the temptation when faced with a mouthwatering display. I find I am at greatest risk of filling my basket if I am the slightest bit hungry.

8.   If you are tempted to buy something extra, do make sure to fit it into your weekly plan, otherwise it will sit in your fridge and make its way to the back.

9.   Work your list in order of the supermarket layout. This way you buy less and avoid the aisles that provoke the "can I haves?". You also get to the check-out quicker.

10. Don't buy something because it has trendy packaging, a nice bottle or is served from a pretty bowl.

11. Don't buy anything that is not on your list, unless you see an exceptional bargain in something you use regularly.

12. Don't forget to take your list and shopping bags.

13. When you have unpacked your shopping, return the bags to the boot of the car or hang them up on the back of the door.

14. Meat will keep well in the fridge for five days. Fish will keep for two or three days if fresh when purchased. If in doubt, use the freezer.

Store cupboard

The store-cupboard list looks very long but you will be surprised how much of it you already have. Check through your cupboards and tick off what you do have and add the rest to your shopping list.

Almonds, slivered 100g
Allspice
Anchovies, salted
Bay leaves
Bulgar wheat, 175g
Capers
Caraway seeds
Cardamom pods
Chickpeas – 3 x 400g tin
  or 600g dried
Chillies, dried whole
Chilli powder
Chilli sauce, sweet
Cider/wine vinegar
Cinnamon sticks x 2
Cinnamon, ground
Cloves, ground
Cloves, whole
Coconut milk, 3 x tins
Coriander, ground or seeds
Cornflour
Couscous
Cumin seeds
Curry powder,
  desired strength
Fennel seeds
Fenugreek
Gherkins
Ginger, ground

Honey
Horseradish cream/sauce
  (cream is best)
Juniper berries
Kidney beans, 1 x 400g tin
Marsala
Martini/Vermouth
Mayonnaise
Mint jelly
Mustard, plain Dijon
Mustard, wholegrain
Noodles, egg 2 packets
Noodles, rice 2 packets
Nutmeg, whole
Oregano, dried
Olive oil
Paprika, smoked
Peanut butter
Pearl barley, 200g
Pepper, black
Peppercorns, whole
Pinenuts, 120g
Porridge oats, 100g
Prunes, 750g
Pumpkin seeds, 250g
Puy lentils, 350g
Raisins, 350g
Redcurrant jelly
Red lentils, 250g

Rice, organic/short grain,
  3.25kg
Rice, risotto (same as
  pudding), 600g
Rose-water
Saffron, Spanish
Salt, Maldon
Salt, sea
Self-raising flour (optional)
Sour cherries, dried 200g
Soy sauce or tamari
Spaghetti or pasta of
  choice 2 x 500g pack
Sugar, brown
Sugar, regular
Sunflower seeds
Turmeric
Tomato chutney or relish
Tomato ketchup
Tomato purée/concentrate
Tomatoes tinned 14 x 400g
Vegetable oil
Vermouth
Wine, red
Wine, white

Oven Temperatures

Remember all ovens give different heat and it is important to get to know your own. I have five different ovens and they vary a lot in temperature. 140°C in one is cool but in another it is moderate. Oven temperatures are guides so just like timing don't get too bogged down with it all. Remember to test your oven and check the food as it cooks and adjust the temperature to suit.

	°C	Gas
very cool	110–120	¼–½
cool	140–150	1–2
moderate	160–180	3–4
moderately hot	190–200	5–6
hot	210–230	7–8
very hot	240–250	9

All recipes are for 4 people unless otherwise stated.

Basics

Brown Soda Scones

We are not eating enough brown bread. This recipe has no white flour and has a handful of seeds added, so it's packed with goodness. Makes about 26 scones and freezes really well, so there is no waste.

500g coarse brown flour

500g fine brown flour

1tsp bread soda

1tsp baking powder

A handful of seeds, pumpkin
and sunflower

1 egg

3tbsp olive oil

600–700ml buttermilk

Some extra fine brown flour for
dusting and cutting the scones

Heat the oven to 250°/Gas 9 or its hottest.

Mix all the dry ingredients together.

In a bowl beat the egg and add the olive oil and a little buttermilk (to loosen mixture).

Add the egg mixture to the dry ingredients and enough of the buttermilk to bind. (I like my mixture to be a little wet, sticky to the touch.) Sprinkle with flour before turning out, to stop it sticking to your hands.

Flour your work surface, turn out the dough and sprinkle with a little more flour so it is not sticky to the touch. Press into shape with your hand, about 1cm thick, not working it too much. No need for a rolling pin.

Cut in scone shapes and put on a floured baking tray.

Bake in the hot oven for about 12–15 minutes. Cool on a rack.

Notes

Great to eat on the day and the next, otherwise freeze once they have cooled down. They defrost within a couple of hours in a warm kitchen. I like to take them out at night and have them for breakfast.

Good Things White Loaf

Please give this bread recipe a go; you will be delighted with the result.
We make 4kg of it every morning in the restaurant and also use the dough to make
our Durrus cheese, spinach and nutmeg pizza (see page 300).

500g white bread flour, also
known as strong flour
1 x 7g sachet (2tsp) instant
dried yeast
2½tsp salt
350ml lukewarm water –
not hot, not cold

In a large mixing bowl, mix the flour, yeast and salt together. Next add in almost all the water and mix well with a wooden spoon to form a dough. Continue mixing until the dough has come together and the bowl is clean. If your dough is a little dry, add the remaining water and if it is a little sticky add a little more flour.

Generously flour your work surface and turn the dough out on to it. Knead the dough for about 10 minutes, until it is soft, springy and clean. You might need to sprinkle a little flour as you go. Sprinkle flour if the dough is sticking to your hands or the surface – your hands should be clean of dough as you work. This should be a relaxed affair, so don't overwork the dough (you will end up with a heavy loaf and tense shoulders). Place the dough back in the bowl, cover it with cling film and put it somewhere warm, but not hot, for at least an hour in summer and two in winter.

Once the dough has doubled in size and is light with a few little bubbles on top, tip it out on to the floured surface, give it a quick knead and shape it into a round ball. Then place it on a floured baking sheet. Dust it with flour (I like to use a handful of brown flour here, as it gives the loaf a nice colour) and leave to rise again – this should take from 30 to 45 minutes, depending on the time of year.

Set the oven to 250°C/Gas 9. Do this about 15 minutes before the bread is ready to go in the oven.

Place the bread in the middle of the oven and bake for 20 minutes, then lower the heat to 220°C/Gas 7 and give it another 10 minutes. Do check the bread for doneness by tapping the bottom of the loaf; it should sound hollow. If not, give it another few minutes.

Let the loaf cool on a wire rack.

Notes

For making pizza, the dough will keep in the fridge for 4–5 days, but do remember to bring it to room temperature before rolling out.

Rice

Serves 4–6 people, depending on appetite. I always like to have extra rice in the fridge during the week, so I usually make double the recipe. I know I can make a quick dish for lunch or dinner if I have nothing else planned.

500g organic short
    grain brown rice
Olive oil
2 bay leaves
1 whole head of garlic (whole!!)
Salt and pepper
750ml boiling water

A heavy-based saucepan with
a tight-fitting lid

Boil the kettle.

Heat the saucepan.

Put enough olive oil in the hot saucepan to coat the bottom nicely and add the rice, bay leaf, head of garlic, a good pinch of salt and pepper and mix well to warm the rice for a few minutes. Add the boiling water and season with salt and pepper. Bring to the boil, cover with a lid and cook for about 30–40 minutes on the lowest heat you can manage, without opening the lid. You will not need to drain your rice if you have the right amount of water.

Leave to sit for a few minutes and fork through before serving.

Notes
Rice will keep in the fridge for five days and can be reheated in a hot pan with a little oil in a couple of minutes

Quick rice dishes
Beat two eggs together, heat a wok or frying pan, add a little oil and pour in the egg. Let it cook for a minute (it will set like an omelette), then mix well to break it up. Add the rice and stirfry until the rice is very hot. Add some cooked chopped chicken if you have it and serve with some chilli sauce OR

chop up some leftover cooked chicken, heat a wok to very hot and stirfry the chicken until crisp, add a bag of fresh spinach leaves, chopped, and a splash of water, season with salt and pepper. Add the rice and mix well until everything is very hot.

Bread Rolls (Ideal for Burgers)

Well worth making! Make double the recipe and keep some in the freezer for later. I can never understand why people buy good meat to make burgers and then buy poor-quality rolls. If I don't have any rolls, I often toast thick slices of the bread on page 74 and use them instead.

500g bread (strong) flour

200g fine wholemeal plain flour

1 sachet (2tsp) instant dried yeast

7g (2tsp) salt

1tsp sugar

200ml lukewarm milk, plus a
    little extra for brushing

250ml lukewarm water

Sesame or poppy seeds to
    sprinkle on top

In a large bowl, mix together the flours, yeast, salt and sugar. Add the milk and water and mix with a wooden spoon to form a dough. Turn on to a floured surface and knead for five minutes until the dough is soft and elastic.

Put the dough back into the bowl and cover with cling film. Leave to stand in a warm place for about an hour until it has doubled in size.

Knead the dough again lightly to knock out the air.

Divide the dough into about 10 portions. Shape each one into a round ball, then flatten out a little. Place on floured baking trays, leaving enough room for them to rise. Leave to rise for about 30 minutes until nearly doubled in size.

Press your thumb into the centre of each roll, which will make the surface slightly flat rather than domed. Brush with a little milk and scatter over the seeds.

Preheat the oven to 220°/Gas 7.

Bake in the preheated oven for about 10 minutes until golden. When the base is tapped they should sound hollow.

Transfer to a wire cooling rack, cover with a dry teatowel and leave to cool. This will help to keep them soft rather than crusty.

Couscous

Olive oil
200g couscous
200ml boiling water
Salt

Boil a kettle of water.

Heat a medium saucepan and add a good splash of oil. Add the couscous and toast for two or three minutes in the hot oil without letting it brown until the grains are fragrant. Measure out the boiling water from the kettle and pour over the couscous, mix well, turn off the heat and cover. Let stand for 15 minutes.

Fluff the couscous with a fork and season with more salt if needed. Serve immediately or keep in a warm oven until you are ready to serve it.

Notes

Will keep in the fridge covered for four or five days. Couscous can be reheated, covered, in a medium oven for 20 minutes or tossed in a hot pan with a knob of butter or some olive oil.

Makes a great dessert mixed with melted butter, cinnamon, sugar, some toasted nuts and dried fruit such as sour cherries and raisins and served with a bowl of yoghurt and some fresh limes.

For something a little more interesting, try the almond and raisin recipe on the next page.

Almond and Raisin Couscous

2tbsp butter

200g couscous

200ml boiling water

Salt

½tsp cinnamon

100g raisins

100g whole skinned almonds,
    toasted and chopped,
      or slivered almonds toasted

Boil the kettle.

Heat a medium saucepan and melt the butter.

Add the couscous and nuts and stir over a medium heat for two or three minutes, until the grains are fragrant.

Measure out the boiling water from the kettle.

Add the salt, the cinnamon and the currants; give it a quick stir and pour over the couscous.

Turn off the heat.

Cover the saucepan and let it sit for 15 minutes.

Fluff the couscous with a fork and season with salt if necessary. Serve immediately or hold in a warm oven until you're ready to serve it.

Notes

Quinoa: To avoid wheat, try quinoa – an ancient Inca grain and really good for you. Take 400g of quinoa and boil for 10 minutes in plenty of water, then drain. Make a dressing with olive oil, lemon juice, a little ground cumin, fennel, salt and pepper. Mix into the cooked quinoa. Lovely cold from the fridge.

Gravy

Never panic over making gravy.
Roast your joint on a blazing high heat ("stewing" the roast on a medium
heat draws out the fat, which spoils the gravy). Caramelisation from high heat
deepens the flavour and browns the gravy to perfection.
Place a mixture of vegetables and herbs under the roast to flavour the gravy. All you
need to do then is simply add water (potato water from the cooked vegetables is
brilliant) and a few other subtle, simple flavourings and let nature take its course.
Out go foil, racks, flour and any artificial "browning" ingredient.

1 whole unpeeled head of garlic
2 onions, skins left on, quartered
2 celery sticks
1 carrot
Sprigs of thyme
4 bay leaves
Salt and pepper

Preheat your oven to its maximum temperature. Roughly chop all the vegetables and place all these ingredients into a low-sided oven roasting tray along with the herbs and seasoning. Season your roast. Place the roast on top of the vegetables and herbs, and put into the preheated oven for 30 minutes. The oven must be very hot at this stage to caramelise the meat and the vegetables, which will sweeten and colour the gravy. Turn the heat down to approximately 200°C/Gas 6. Roast according to the size and cut of your joint of meat. When cooked, remove from the oven and set the joint to rest.

The vegetables and herbs should be brown and caramelised. For pork you might add a sliced cooking apple and sliced ginger. For chicken, it's a good idea to place a lemon inside the cavity, which will give a lovely flavour to the gravy.

Place the oven tray directly on to the hob and scrape the juices free over a medium heat.

You can add Marsala, whiskey (great with roast duck), apple juice (for pork), tomatoes, vegetable water or just tap water. Season the gravy with salt and freshly ground pepper. Squash the vegetables into the sauce, especially the garlic, to get the most out of their flavour.

Leave the gravy to cook over a relatively high heat for at least five minutes.

Strain directly into your gravy boat and here, in minutes, is perfect delicious gravy.

Mashed Potatoes

1kg potatoes, peeled
Salt
Water

Stage 1

Bring a kettle of water to the boil, chop the potatoes to roughly the same size and fit snugly into a saucepan.

Pour over just enough boiling water to cover the potatoes.

Add a good pinch of salt.

Boil with a lid on for 15 to 20 minutes until fully cooked through. Check by cutting a potato in half; it should be soft and dry.

Drain the potatoes well, keeping back the water.

Leave in the colander over the empty saucepan for a few minutes to dry out; you may need to have the heat on low for this. If you don't dry the potatoes, you will have a heavy mash.

While still very hot, mash the potatoes using a potato masher, a vegetable mouli or a potato ricer. Do not use any electric gadget, as they overwork the potatoes and make them too starchy.

At this stage you can cool and store the mashed potatoes in the fridge (they keep for five days) and use for any of the dishes listed below. Or continue to finish off, following Stage 2, for immediate use.

Uses for mashed potatoes after Stage 1

To top a meat, fish or vegetable pie
Fish cakes – page 170
Potato cake – page 39
Fish pie – page 144

½ pint of cream, milk and potato water (cream is optional)

Salt and pepper – to taste

100g butter or olive oil or a mixture of both or do without!

Stage 2

In the now empty pot, add the cream or milk and bring to the boil.

Add the mashed potatoes and mix well, making sure they are piping hot. If your potatoes are cold from the fridge, this will take about 3 to 4 minutes.

If the mash is too stiff, add a little of the potato water or milk.

Taste, season with salt and pepper. Add a knob of butter if you like.

Potato Cake

500g potatoes, peeled
   (for 2 people)
Olive oil
Butter
Salt and pepper

20cm ovenproof frying pan
Slicer, such as a mandoline

Preheat the oven to its hottest.

Heat the frying pan on a medium heat. When warm add a good splash of oil and a knob of butter.

Melt together and coat the base and the sides of the pan with the mixture.

Pour off any excess fat and keep in a bowl until later.

Keeping the pan on the heat, start slicing the potatoes.

They need to be very thin, but not so thin you don't get a complete slice.

Layer the potatoes in the pan, going around in a clockwise direction and working your way into the middle. Making sure you are spreading them evenly, leaving no gap.

Season with salt and pepper every third layer.

You want to finish with a nice thick cake, so you will have a contrast of crisp and soft potato.

You might need to add another potato.

Brush the top with the reserved oil mixture, place in the middle of the oven and bake for 20 to 30 minutes or until the potatoes are soft when tested with a knife.

Flip the cake out on to a plate or chopping board and slide back topside down into the pan.

Return to the oven or put on a medium flame for a few minutes.

Turn out, cut into wedges and serve.

Notes

Do not keep the sliced potatoes in water, as you will lose the starch. You need this for the potatoes to stick together.

To make into a complete meal

Add some sliced cheese around the halfway stage, along with some chopped thyme. Serve with some cooked spinach and a fried or poached egg. I like to use a semi-soft cheese. A great way to use up bits and pieces lying around in the fridge is to lightly cook a couple of slices of bacon and add with some cheese to the middle.

Or try a mixture of chopped anchovies, capers, thyme and lemon zest and serve with some grilled or pan-fried fish.

Roast Potatoes

250–350g potatoes per person

Boil the kettle. Place a flat-sided oven tray in the oven and heat it to its hottest.

Peel and chop the largest potatoes to resemble the smallest one. Fit the potatoes snugly in a saucepan and just cover with boiling water.

Cover with a tight-fitting lid and bring to the boil, reduce the heat and cook the potatoes for five to seven minutes or until they are just a little soft on the outside but still very hard in the middle.

Drain, reserve the water. Return the potatoes to the saucepan to dry out, giving them a good shake to help them along and to fluff up the outside of the potatoes.

Pour in a good splash of oil, just enough to coat the potatoes evenly, and season well with salt.

Remove the hot tray from the oven and spread out the oiled potatoes evenly. Return to the oven and roast for 15 to 25 minutes, depending on their size.

Notes

Keep the potato water for making a gravy, soup or the bread on page 26.

Basic Tomato Sauce

This recipe gives you two portions. If you increased this recipe threefold you would have the basis for six quick dishes (see list on opposite page).

30ml (2tbsp) olive oil

3 large onions, finely chopped

3 carrots, finely chopped

3 celery sticks, cleaned and
    finely chopped

2 x 400g tins tomatoes, whole
    or chopped

4 cloves of garlic, chopped

Mixture of herbs, something
    like a little chopped
    rosemary, a small sprig of
    thyme and a bunch of parsley,
    or just some parsley

Salt and black pepper

Take a pan with a tight-fitting lid and heat to medium.
Add the oil to the pan, followed by the onions, carrots and celery, turning them to coat in oil. Add the rosemary and thyme (if you have them) along with the stalks of the parsley and season well with salt and pepper. Mix well. Cook the vegetables for about five minutes until they soften a little. Now cook on a very low heat with the lid on for at least 20 minutes. Add tomatoes, garlic and the parsley leaves and simmer on a low heat until thick and pulpy, about 30 minutes. Mix well during cooking to prevent sticking and help to crush the tomatoes. Taste and season if needed.
You can purée the sauce or leave chunky.
Keep in the fridge for four or five days or freeze in two batches, which will give you sauce for two recipes during the month ahead.

Notes

When making a batch for your freezer, make at least this amount and double if you have a saucepan big enough. It will make your life easier during the next month.

I only use fresh tomatoes for a sauce if I have some that really need using up or I end up with a lot from a grower.

One of the best things about making a tomato sauce is I get to use up those bits and pieces in the fridge. When we close the café after the summer I make big batches with the vegetables we have left over and freeze it for the winter to feed my family.

I do not stick to the above recipe; I make it by eye and use onions, leeks, celery, carrots, fennel, red peppers, all the fresh herbs we have left and a few big tins of tomatoes.

The uses for tomato sauce in the book

Ratatouille – see page 240

Fish stew – see page 99

Fish pie – see page 144

Fish soup – see page 266

Tomato, caper and herb sauce with pan-fried fish –
see page 195

Stolen Cuban dish – see page 174

Moussaka – see page 221

To purée or not to purée

I used to purée all my sauce when the children were
younger but now I don't bother. I'm not sure if I got lazy and
intolerant or they got less fussy. I also discovered more
things to do with it not puréed.

Other uses for tomato sauce

Pizza

Pasta

Tomato soup

Serve as a sauce with steak, chicken, pork or fish

Peperonata

Pan-fried sausages slow-cooked in tomato sauce

Salads and their dressings

Salad with dressing is so simple but we have made it very complicated. Our problem is we have too many oils, vinegars and salads on offer, so we don't know where to start.

Eating a green salad with every meal became part of my life when I lived in France 25 years ago. It was so simple. You had one oil, usually from the area, some vinegar, mustard and sea salt.

I still eat a salad every day of the year, but it is not always green. Why buy bags or heads of salad leaves in winter which are over-priced and tasteless? These leaves need lots of dressing and extra bits added in to make them interesting. So why not make salads with what is in season, grown locally, that tastes good in its own right?

It is winter as I write this and I am making salads with beetroot, red, white and green cabbage, carrots, turnips, celery, apples, oranges, white and red onions. The secret to making these ingredients work is getting the right combination, matching them with the main dish and getting the dressing right. As we have such a range of oils and vinegars, our winter salads need never be boring.

You need to get the balance of ingredients right and the best way to achieve this is to taste as you put it together. The simpler you keep the salad, the nicer the end result will be. Too many flavours never work well in the one dish.

When matching a salad with a main dish I always think what is the classic accompaniment for it. For instance, with pork with apple sauce, red cabbage and cider, I will serve an apple and cabbage salad dressed with some oil, cider vinegar and a good pinch of mixed spice.

When I serve a spicy main course I like to make a salad with sliced onions, which I cover in boiling water for a couple of minutes to retain their crispness while banishing their aggression. I mix in some chopped parsley or coriander and dress it with olive oil and lemon juice. When eating fish I keep my salads very simple, making sure the flavours of the fish are not spoilt. Here, some green salad leaves simply dressed with good olive oil and sea salt is all that is needed. When you are not luckly enough to get good green salad try a salad of tomatoes, olives, some fresh parsley (dill, fennel or chervil) and dress it with some olive oil, lemon juice and sea salt.

I have no recipe for a salad dressing; my guide is taste. The rule for making a dressing is usually 2:1 but this does not always work as it will depend on the flavour of your oil and the sharpness of the vinegar. I don't want it too strong or it will overpower the salad and take from the flavour of the main course. It is so important to taste the dressing as you make it, especially for the vinegars and seasoning. The oil is the carrier for the other ingredients so plays an important part in the dressing; it should not have a bitter taste. When I have a flavourless oil I use

it as the base for a strong dressing such as mustard or honey. To oils bursting with flavour I add as little as possible, more often than not just some good sea salt such as Maldon and the odd time a splash of vinegar. I find the better the vinegar the more oil I need to use, especially when I use balsamic, which tends to be sweet.

The most important ingredient is the oil, be it olive, pumpkin, nut or sunflower it should have a pleasant taste and most importantly be to your liking. The buying of oils and vinegars has become as mind-boggling as buying wine. Which oil, what country, type of olives and should we get white or red wine, sherry, balsamic or cider vinegar? My advice is to buy what you like and stick with it. We now have a big choice of vinegars, like oils. Good cider vinegar is the one I use mostly and then I always have a nice bottle of balsamic.

When buying balsamic take a moment to read the label. A lot of them are white wine vinegar with colouring and additives and often we are paying for a pretty bottle.

I always use undistilled cider vinegar, the cloudy type. Besides cooking, it has many other uses in my house as it is a natural antibiotic. I use it for sore throats, burns and I very often make a drink with two tablespoons of vinegar in hot water and a little local honey to start the day.

Making a dressing can be fun and it will taste different every time you make it. Children love to make dressings and it is a great way to get them to eat salads.

Fish Stock

Use the debris left from preparing firm white fish such as turbot, brill, sole, monk or John Dory. Fish shops will be delighted to give them to you, but you may have to give them a day's notice, as they fillet early in the morning. Avoid bones from oily fish such as mackerel, salmon and herring.

1kg fish trimmings,
    bones and heads
1 onion, sliced
1 celery stick, chopped
4 parsley stalks
4 sprigs of thyme
1 bay leaf
½tbsp black peppercorns
2½–3litres of tap water

Fill the sink with cold water, add the bones and give them a quick wash.

Put all the ingredients into a large pan and cover with cold water.

Bring to the boil, skimming off any scum that rises to the surface.

Simmer very gently for 40 minutes.

Strain through a fine sieve and leave to cool.

Use or freeze stock as required.

Freezing stock for the recipes in the book

500ml for fish stew on page 99.

500ml for fish pie on page 144.

175ml for monkfish on page 120.

200ml for pan-fried fish on page 195.

200ml for braised fennel on page 217.

I find used washed-out milk and cream cartons ideal for this. They have lids and the 500ml cream cartons are particularly good. Will keep in the freezer for two months.

Chicken Stock

2 cooked chicken carcasses
and bones
The neck and giblets from the
chicken but not the liver
1–2 onions, roughly chopped
1–2 large carrots, roughly
chopped
3–4 celery sticks, roughly
chopped
½ large leek, roughly chopped
2 bay leaves
A few peppercorns
Any herbs you can get
2 litres of water

Put the carcasses, along with any skin, bones, fat or jelly from the roasting tin, into a saucepan that will take them snugly. If you have the fresh giblets, add these too (minus the liver, which can make the stock bitter). Add the vegetables and herbs, packing them in as snugly as you can so that you need no more than 2 litres of cold water just to cover everything.

Bring the pan to a simmer and let it cook, uncovered, for at least two hours and up to five. Top up the water once or twice, as necessary. Strain the stock through a fine sieve, leave it to cool and chill. A layer of fat will solidify on top, which you can scrape off, but I don't usually bother unless there's a lot of it. The stock will keep in the fridge for four or five days and will freeze really well for at least 3 months.

Notes

You can make a stock with one carcass and half the rest of the ingredients. I prefer to wait until I have two; I stick them in the freezer after the Sunday roast. Sometimes if I need a stock and only have one carcass I get a small beef and pork bone from the butcher to add some extra flavour. Roast them for 30 minutes in a hot oven before adding to the stockpot.

List of dishes using chicken stock

1 litre for lemon and pinenut risotto on page 105.
1 litre for topside of beef on page 119.
250ml for sausages with juniper and Marsala on page 123.
1 litre for mushroom risotto on page 152.
1 litre for barley, potato and chicken stew on page 244.

* All chicken stock can be replaced with vegetable stock, see page 50.

Vegetable Stock

Always handy to have in the freezer. Easy to make as you collect bits of vegetables and their peelings. If you are not cooking daily for a vegetarian, it can always be used instead of a meat stock for a risotto or noodle dish or to finish off a quick supper dish.

2 medium onions, chopped
2 medium carrots, chopped
2 celery sticks, chopped
Any trimmings from leeks,
    fennel and herb stalks
2 bay leaves
Salt and pepper

Put all the vegetables and herbs in a saucepan and cover with water.
Bring to the boil and simmer for 40 minutes.
Season with salt and pepper.
Cool, strain and store.

Notes
Stock will keep in the fridge for five days and will keep in the freezer for only one month. Do not use potatoes, parsnips, turnips or sweet potatoes in a stock.

Winter

Week 1

Recipes

Shopping List

Supermarket

Pitta bread or bread
  (for burger)
750g frozen spinach
750ml pure apple juice
  or cider

Vegetables & Fruit

4 kg potatoes
4 large baking potatoes
9 onions
2 garlic
6 carrots
1 red cabbage (about 1kg)
12 medium flat or chestnut
  mushrooms
1 head of celery
2 leeks
1 green cabbage
1 fresh raw beetroot
1 red onion
1 bunch of spring onions

4 lemons
3 limes
7 cooking apples
About 2cm fresh ginger
3 ripe tomatoes
Salad leaves for 4 people
3 bunches parsley
2 bunches coriander, optional
1 cucumber

Dairy

Large tub natural yoghurt
  (500ml)
½ dozen eggs
1 small packet of butter

Fish Shop

4 x 250g plaice (fillets)
500g (undyed) smoked
  haddock or unsmoked fish

Butcher

3kg shoulder of pork on the
  bone (might need to order
  in advance)
800g lean minced beef
2kg lamb neck chops
  on bone

Other Shopping

Weekend Work for Week 1

This is the first weekend work list, so it is important to get into a routine. After you have put away your shopping and cleared your work space, move away any unwanted objects that are not to do with your work list and get started. This work list will not take you longer than an hour in the kitchen and you will be set up for the week.

Firstly turn your oven on to heat up and make the bread first. While the bread is baking put on the rice and then prepare the potatoes. Bribe somebody to help you to do the potatoes (a piece of chocolate works wonders for my children). Make a pot of tea, have a glass of wine or listen to the radio and it will not feel like a chore.

Instead of buying rolls for the burgers give the rolls on page 31 a go. I find if I do all my potato work together I get the messy part over with at the weekend and when potatoes are prepared in advance dinnertime seems less of a task.

Some weekends I like to make double the recipe of rice and have extra in the fridge for a quick lunch.

1 recipe of soda scones (page 25)
- *Put in the freezer when cooled down, keeping some back for the weekend.*

1½ recipe of mashed potatoes (page 37–8)
- *Also prepare the potatoes for the chips on page 74. Keep them covered with water in the fridge (this is good for them, as they lose some of the starch which causes them to stick to the tray).*

1 recipe of rice (page 29)
- *for the kedgeree on page 70.*

Plaice in a Bag with Horseradish and Potatoes

Even if you are not a horseradish fan, do give this a try as it works so well.
A quick simple dish in which you can use any fish you like, but I find plaice works
really well here. It is not expensive and you can use up leftover boiled potatoes.
You can make this a complete meal in a bag, so do add more potatoes if you need to.
This will take you just 10 minutes to get ready.

Olive oil

4 large cooked potatoes
(more if needed), sliced

2tbsp horseradish cream
or sauce

¼ medium cucumber, sliced
thinly

4 plaice fillets – about 250g
each in weight

1 large lemon, washed and
sliced thinly

Salt and pepper

A few sprigs of fresh dill, fennel
or parsley (if you have it),
roughly chopped

4 sheets of greaseproof or
baking parchment, about
50cm in length

Turn your oven to its highest temperature and heat two oven trays. DO THIS BEFORE YOU START ANYTHING ELSE.
Spread out your four sheets of greaseproof or parchment, lightly brush the surface with olive oil.
Lay the sliced potatoes in the centre in the bottom half of the paper. Now spread the horseradish cream over the potatoes with a knife (do this to taste). Lay the slices of cucumber on top and season a little with salt and pepper. Next lay the fish on top, season lightly, top with a couple of slices of lemon and sprinkle with some chopped herbs.
Fold the paper over the fish and seal up the sides really well. You must start with a knot at one corner and continue to knot all the way to the other side, making sure it is well sealed.
With an oven cloth remove the hot trays from the oven and place the fish parcels on them, making sure they are not overlapping.
Bake for about six to seven minutes. Remove from the oven and place each bag on a plate and let everybody open their own so they will experience the lovely smell.

Notes

Parchment looks better than foil but foil is easier to seal up and we nearly always have it in the kitchen.

Peel the potatoes if you like. I couldn't be bothered, and why not eat the skin – it's good for us.

If you are not a cucumber fan, they are nicer cooked.

You could use courgette instead.

Unwaxed lemons are best if you can find them.

Herbs are not essential for this dish.

Instead of making four packets, make one large one the size of the oven tray and seal up well.

Roast Shoulder of Pork with Gravy, Mashed Potatoes and Braised Red Cabbage

Shoulder of pork on the bone is usually something you need to order a little in advance from your butcher, as it is a very slow seller – which I find hard to understand, as it is great value and the best cut for roasting and you cannot mess it up!!!

3kg shoulder of pork
   on the bone with the skin
   scored
2 large onions, roughly chopped
   with the skins on
3 celery sticks, roughly sliced
2 carrots, roughly chopped
3 cooking apples, roughly
   chopped (don't peel or core)
6 or 8 bay leaves
750ml apple juice or cider
Salt and pepper
Mashed potatoes (page 37)
Braised red cabbage (page 69)

Heat the oven to the hottest for at least 20 minutes. DO THIS BEFORE YOU DO ANYTHING ELSE. Take a roasting tray or a frying pan that is suitable to go in the oven (no plastic or wood – the smell is not very nice). You want it to fit the joint nicely. On the bottom of your roasting tray pile up all your vegetables and apples, season well with salt and pepper and sprinkle the bay leaves on top.

Sit the pork on top of the vegetables (some will be exposed; this is good). Sprinkle with salt and pepper and place in the middle of the very hot oven.

For the next half hour or so you will need to keep watch. Turn the heat down when the skin is nicely brown and crisp. This can take anything from 20 to 45 minutes, depending on your oven. I find fan ovens rather powerful and things seem to happen quickly.

When this has happened, turn your heat down to 160°/Gas 3 and roast for four hours; if you leave it longer it will come to no harm. You can do this at a lower temperature for longer if it suits you. If you have room in the oven you can cook the red cabbage happily in the bottom of the oven for two or three hours or even a little longer.

Prepare the potatoes for mash if not already in the fridge. The vegetables under your roast will be slightly burnt looking, but this will give your gravy colour. If some are very burnt, remove them. They should be a mixture of mushy and caramelised.

To make the gravy, remove the meat to a large plate and keep in a warm place, leaving the vegetables in the tray. Pour off any excess fat as you hold back the vegetables. Put your roasting tray on the hob over a medium heat and give everything a good stir up, scraping off any sticky bits – this will add sweetness to your gravy. Do this for about a minute. Pour in the bottle of apple juice or cider, adding enough water to cover the vegetables. Bring the tray up to the boil, turn the heat down and let it simmer for at least 10 minutes. Taste from time to time and season if necessary while the gravy is simmering.

You can now start carving the meat. Remove the crackling and cut into pieces, then slice the meat – really it will just fall apart for you. Put it on a large serving plate topped with the crackling.

To finish the gravy, strain it through a sieve – giving everything a good squeeze – and serve.

Serve with mashed potato and red cabbage.

Notes

This is my favourite dish if I am cooking for a large number of people. I usually cook the joint overnight in the oven. I like to cook a bigger piece, as I love to feed a lot of people together and I like leftovers. So I cook a whole shoulder, which can be anything from 5 to 10kg. I give it 45 minutes to 1 hour at a high heat then lower the oven to 140–150°C/Gas1–2. The house smells lovely in the morning. I put it in the oven about 8pm the evening before and it is ready for lunch at 1pm the next day or later if I need it.

If your oven has room and you decide to make roast potatoes, use the reserved fat from the pork.

Planning ahead

1. *Keep about 250g pork and some gravy for a stirfry on page 73.*
2. *Freeze about 500g (or 250g to go with 250g of cooked beef on page 119) of the leftover cooked meat to make meat sauce for pasta (page 127).*
3. *If you have any left you can make a sandwich, with some good relish or gherkins.*

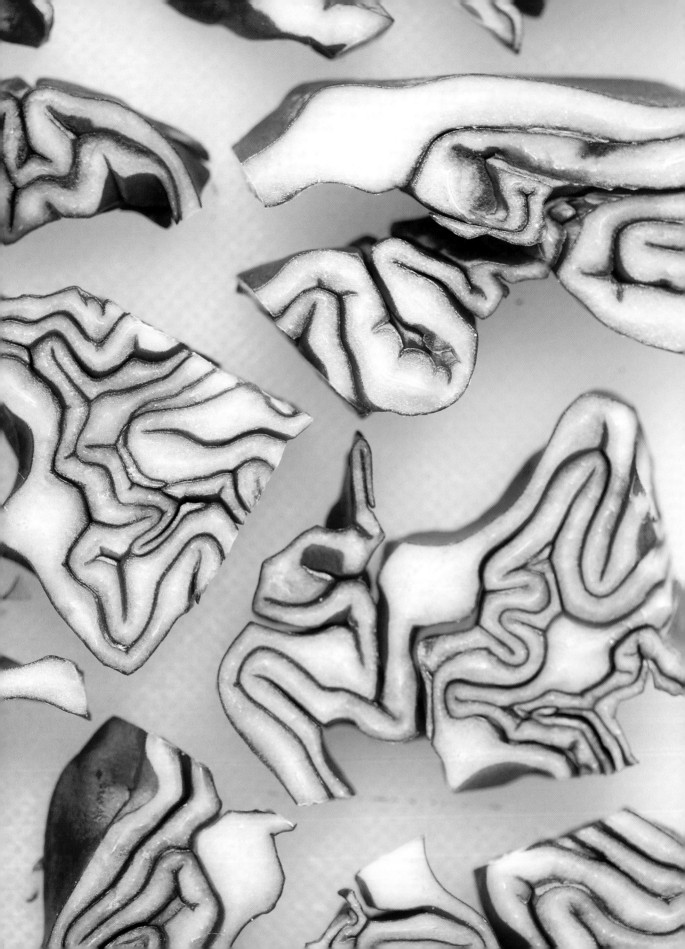

Braised Red Cabbage

1kg red cabbage

2 large onions, peeled and sliced

4 cooking apples or sour
  eating apples, peeled, cored
  and sliced

½ tsp ground cinnamon

½ tsp ground cloves

½ tsp ground coriander

½ tsp ground ginger

Good few gratings of nutmeg

2 tbsp brown sugar

3 tbsp cider vinegar

Salt and pepper

Heat the oven to 150°/Gas 2 and cook for two hours.
Remove the outer leaves of the cabbage. Halve and chop
as finely as you can (keep at least two handfuls back for later
in the week).
Place in a heavy-based saucepan with a tight-fitting lid, along
with the other ingredients, and mix well with your hands.
Cook for two hours at the above temperature (or three hours
with the slow-roasting pork).
Alternatively you can cook it on the hob on a very low heat.

Notes
Red cabbage is great reheated and freezes well.

Planning ahead
*Keep some red cabbage back for the noodle dish later in the
week; cover well in the fridge.*

Kedgeree

2 eggs, hard boiled and
    quartered
Olive oil
1 medium onion, finely chopped
Salt and pepper
1 clove of garlic, finely chopped
2 heaped teaspoons curry
    powder or to your taste
500g undyed smoked haddock
    fillets, skinned, pinboned and
    cut into bite-sized pieces
2 bay leaves
Salt and pepper
2 lemons, 1 juiced and
    1 quartered
2 good handfuls of fresh
    coriander, roughly chopped

650g cooked short grain brown
    rice (see page 29)

Heat the olive oil in a large frying pan or wok over a low heat and add the onion, garlic and bay leaves. Allow to soften without colouring for about five minutes, then add the curry powder and cook for a couple of minutes more.

Next add the smoked haddock and cook for about one minute. Add the lemon juice.

Add the rice to the pan and gently heat through, then add half the coriander and stir in gently. Taste and add more lemon juice and seasoning if needed.

Put into a warm serving dish (or leave in the frying pan) and serve with the quartered lemon and egg arranged around the dish. Sprinkle with the rest of the coriander. Serve with a green salad dressed with sea salt and good olive oil.

Notes

If you cannot get undyed smoked fish, use fresh haddock or pollock.

You can use leftover cooked chicken instead of fish.

You could make it a vegetable dish by using a mixture of seasonal vegetables. In the winter a mixture of carrots, turnip and parsnip works well.

Noodles with
Peanut Dressing and Pork

This dish is known in our house as peanut butter stirfry. I secretly call it empty the fridge dish.

1 medium onion, sliced thinly

2 celery sticks, sliced thinly

12 medium mushrooms

Salt and pepper

2cm finger of fresh ginger, peeled and grated

4 fat cloves of garlic, chopped

Salt and pepper

A splash of leftover gravy

1 packet of rice noodles

For the peanut sauce, mix together

2tbsp of peanut butter

3tbsp of sweet chilli sauce – from a bottle

2tbsp of Tamari or soy sauce

Juice of 3 limes

Sliced cooked pork

Two good handfuls of raw red cabbage, kept from earlier in the week

3 spring onions, sliced

½ cucumber, cut in sticks

Some fresh coriander

Prepare the noodles as on the packet – I do this just in time to serve hot from the saucepan, then I avoid the rinsing and reheating.

Slice all the vegetables and grate the ginger on a plate.

Mix together all the ingredients for the sauce, mixing well.

Get your wok or frying pan as hot as you can. Add a splash of oil, throw in the onions and celery and cook for about three minutes. Season with salt and pepper.

Keeping the heat high, add the mushrooms and cook for two minutes.

Add the ginger and garlic to the wok, stir in and add a splash of gravy.

In a big serving bowl, pile up the noodles topped with the contents of the wok.

Lay the sliced meat on top and scatter with the red cabbage, spring onions, cucumber and coriander.

Notes

You can use egg noodles. I find rice noodles easier to eat and they have a nicer texture.

I have been trying various brands of noodles and they all seem to have different cooking instructions, so follow the instructions on the packet.

Leave out the mushrooms and use peppers.

Leave out the meat for vegetarians.

Great way of using up bits in the fridge – cucumber, herbs, green cabbage, fennel.

Burgers and Chips

Chips

Around 800g–1kg Red Roosters
Olive oil
Salt and pepper

Burgers

800g lean minced beef
Salt and pepper

Salad and sauces

3 very ripe tomatoes, sliced
1 red onion, halved and
    sliced thinly
1 small beetroot, peeled and
    grated
Some nice salad leaves
¼ cucumber
4 gherkins
Mayonnaise
Jar of tomato relish, to
    pass around
8 slices of day-old good bread
    (page 26), burger buns
    (page 31) or 4 pitta breads

Set the oven at its highest temperature and heat a low-sided tray. Peel and cut the potatoes to your preferred size; I like the old-fashioned chip cutters. Place in a bowl, fill with water and let the cold tap run into them for about five minutes, mixing them now and again to help wash off the starch. Drain and dry well with a teatowel.

Place in a large mixing bowl, season with salt and pepper, pour enough oil to evenly coat all the chips and mix well. Remove the hot tray from the oven, spread the chips evenly on it and return it to the oven. Cook for about 30 minutes or until nicely brown. Check from time to time, mix well on the tray and pour off any excess oil after 15 minutes.

In the meantime, put the minced beef in a mixing bowl, add a generous amount of salt and pepper and mix very well. Shape into four rounds and flatten to your preferred thickness.

Heat a frying pan, grill or BBQ until very hot. Place the burgers on the hot pan and cook for 5 minutes on the first side without moving them. Turn them over and cook for another minute for rare (this will depend on the thickness) and a little longer for medium.

In the meantime, place all the salads on a large plate and toast the bread. Sometimes I toast just one side.

The oven chips should now be done, so serve up in a bowl lined with a teatowel.

Let everybody build their own burger.

Red Lentils stewed with Tomatoes and Spices, served with Spinach, Baked Potato and Natural Yoghurt

4 large potatoes suitable
    for baking
A large bag of frozen spinach
Juice of 1 lemon
Salt and pepper
Nutmeg
Pot of natural yoghurt
2–3 cloves of garlic

Red lentil stew (page 81)

Heat your oven to the hottest, 250°C/Gas 9.

Wash the potatoes well and place on the middle rack in the oven and bake for about 45 minutes or until done. You want the inside nice and soft and the skin crisp.

Make the lentil stew.

While your stew is simmering, defrost the frozen spinach by putting it in a saucepan with a tablespoon of water.

Cover, and put it on a low heat for at least 10 minutes until it is fully defrosted. Drain as much water as you can from the spinach – I find putting it in a sieve and squeezing it with a wooden spoon works well. Return to the saucepan and add the lemon juice.

Season well with salt, pepper and a few good gratings of nutmeg.

Chop the garlic finely or use a garlic crush. Add to the yoghurt and season with some salt.

Serve the baked potatoes split open with some yoghurt spooned over. Pass around the pot of lentil stew topped with the spinach.

Notes

Those who feel a meal is not a meal without meat could serve some grilled bacon or grilled lamb chops with this.

Red Lentil Stew (Dhal)

I do find lentil stews heavy going and boring, but a Dhal I can eat every day, even cold from the fridge.

250g red lentils

Olive oil

1 medium onion, finely chopped

1tbsp coriander seeds, ground

1tsp cumin seeds, ground

½tsp fennel seeds, ground

½tsp chilli powder, or to
  your taste

1tsp turmeric

4 cloves of garlic, chopped

A strip of cinnamon

1 x 400g tin chopped tomatoes

½ bunch coriander leaves,
  if you can find some

Salt and pepper

2tbsp vinegar

Put the lentils in a pan and cover with water. Bring to the boil and cook until soft, about 15–20 minutes. Drain. They will now look like thick porridge.

While the lentils are cooking, warm a saucepan, add some olive oil and cook the onions first on a medium heat for a couple of minutes, then lower the heat for a further five minutes. Add the spices, mix well and cook for another minute.

Add the garlic, vinegar and the cooked lentils. Add the strip of cinnamon. Next add the tomatoes, bring to the boil, turn down to simmer and cook for 20 minutes.

Taste and season with more salt and pepper if necessary and scatter coriander leaves on top.

Irish Stew with Crusted Dumplings, served with Cabbage

I could not leave out Irish stew, one of those great dishes when done well.
I really like the crusted dumplings idea I got from Delia Smith's Winter Cook Book.
This is best cooked the day before, chilled and reheated.

2kg neck lamb chops on the
    bone (you need the bone
    for flavour)
2 medium onions, peeled and
    quartered
4 carrots, quartered
2 medium leeks, sliced
2 large potatoes, peeled and cut
    into about four
2tbsp pearl barley
Salt and black pepper
A couple of good-looking sprigs
    of thyme
Stalks of a good bunch of
    parsley, finely chopped
750ml water

Take a good-sized saucepan that will fit all the ingredients. Season the lamb with salt and pepper and add to the saucepan along with the chopped vegetables, parsley stalks and thyme. Add more salt and pepper and mix everything well together.

Pour in the water, bring everything to the boil and turn down to a simmer. Cook for at least two hours or until the meat is falling off the bone.

If you are doing this the day before, let it cool and put it in the fridge.

For the dumplings:

Dumplings are not suitable for coeliacs unless you use gluten-free flour

175g self-raising flour

The leaves of the bunch of fresh parsley, chopped

75g butter, cold and grated on a coarse grater

Salt and freshly milled black pepper

A lot of chopped parsley to sprinkle at the end

Serve with

1 small head of cabbage (next page)

750g potatoes

Next day

Preheat the oven to 200°/Gas 8.

Take the stew from the fridge and remove any fat that has settled on the top.

Reheat gently and make the dumplings.

Mix the flour and parsley with a seasoning of salt and pepper in a bowl, then mix in – but do not rub in – the grated butter. Now add just sufficient cold water to make fairly stiff but elastic dough that leaves the bowl clean. Shape into 12 dumplings.

When the stew is heated, place the dumplings all over the surface, put the saucepan in the middle of the oven (without a lid) for about 30 minutes until the dumplings are nicely browned and the liquid a little reduced.

While the stew is browning, boil some potatoes and cabbage.

Notes

You can increase the amount of vegetables but not the potatoes. This dish freezes well.

84

Boiled Cabbage

500g green cabbage or
    spring greens
Salt and pepper
Olive oil

Bring a medium pan of water to the boil.
Quarter the cabbage and roughly chop.
Add the cabbage to the boiling water and boil for three to five
minutes or to your liking.
Drain, return to the saucepan and add a splash of olive oil
and some salt and pepper.

Week 2

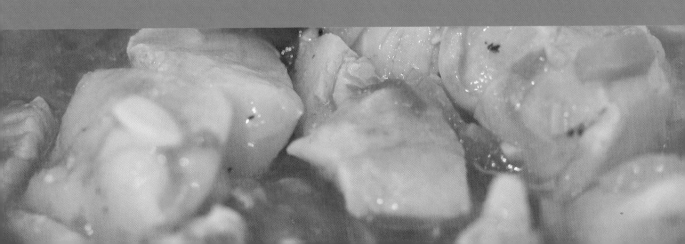

Recipes

Shopping List

Supermarket

Tomato purée
1 x 400g tin chickpeas
750g frozen runner beans
100g streaky bacon
100g pinenuts
Jar of pesto
Bag of frozen peas (750g)

Vegetables & Fruit

7kg potatoes
10 onions
2 garlic bulbs
10 carrots
1kg parsnips
1kg sweet potatoes
4 leeks
1 cauliflower (small)
8 big flat brown mushrooms
1 cabbage (if none left from
  last week)
1 fresh red chilli
2 lemons

2 limes
3 bunches parsley
basil – optional
Fresh mint or coriander
(optional)

Dairy

500ml natural yoghurt
  (large tub)
250g Durrus or unsmoked
  Gubbeen cheese or a
  semi-soft cheese
100g Parmesan cheese
Butter, small pack

Fish Shop

4 x 250g hake fillets
750g haddock or pollock fillets
A very large bag of fish bones
  to make stock

Butcher

3kg shoulder of lamb, boned
  and butterflied
1kg stewing beef (thickly
  sliced)
4 boneless pork loin chops
A mixture of bones to make a
  stock (see page 51) or
  make a vegetable stock
  (see page 52)

Other Shopping

Weekend Work for Week 2

This is the busiest list in all of the eight weeks, but you will be well stocked for the weeks ahead. It will not take you longer than two and a half hours.

Do remember, if you are making the stocks, to pick up the bones when you go shopping. You might have to order them in advance.

As this is going to be a busy couple of hours it is important to plan it well, so start off by making both stocks. When you chop the vegetables for the stocks also chop the vegetables for the tomato sauce, so while your stocks are simmering your sauce will also be under way. Next heat the oven to make the scones and get baking.

While the scones are in the oven prepare the potatoes for the mash; at this stage the fish stock will be ready so you will have more room on the stove. Strain the fish stock and leave to cool. While the potatoes are boiling take off the tomato sauce and allow it to cool. Now cook the rice.

The chicken/meat stock can be simmering away as you tidy up and everything is cooling down. Now prepare the fish dish for this evening.

1 recipe of soda scones (page 25)
> – *Keep some for tomorrow and freeze the rest once they've cooled.*

2 recipes of mash potatoes to the end of Stage 1 (page 37)

1 recipe of tomato sauce (page 44)
> – *one portion for this week, which will keep in the fridge, and freeze the other for Week 4.*

Fish stock (page 49)
> – to go with fish stew on page 99.
> – *Do a large pot and freeze the quantities required on page 49, using milk or cream cartons as containers. You will have the stock in your freezer for the next six weeks of recipes.*

Chicken or vegetable stock (page 51 and page 52)
> – 1 litre needed for risotto on page 105. Freeze the rest.

1 recipe of rice (page 29)
> – to go with fish stew on page 99.

Roast Hake with Parsley, Oregano, Chilli and Lime, served with Leeks and Boiled Potatoes

4 fillets of hake,
  250g each in weight
1–2tbsp olive oil
½tbsp dried oregano
2 good handfuls of fresh
  parsley, chopped
1 medium fresh red chilli,
  deseeded and finely
  chopped
Salt and pepper
2 limes
Potatoes for 4 people (1kg)
3 medium leeks, trimmed,
  washed and sliced

Boil the kettle to cook the potatoes and leeks.

Preheat the oven to 250°/Gas 9 and put in a flat roasting tray to heat up. Put the potatoes on to boil.

Using your hands, rub the olive oil into the hake fillets so that they are very lightly coated. Put the oregano, parsley and chilli into a bowl and mix. Season the hake fillets and pat on the herb mixture.

Put the hake on to the roasting tray – they will sear and sizzle immediately. Add the halved limes to the tray and return to the oven on the top shelf, to slightly colour the top of the fish. Cook for eight minutes. When cooked, serve with the roasted limes, which you can squeeze over the fish.

Serve with potatoes and plain boiled leeks which have been boiled for three minutes.

Planning ahead

If you are doing lamb for tomorrow you need to marinate tonight, (see page 95). If you do not get it done tonight, do it early tomorrow morning.

If you are not using tinned chickpeas, soak some dried ones tonight. 200g dried will yield 400g.

I like to soak extra and make a hummus (see page 304) to have in the fridge for the week for snacks.

Baked Shoulder of Lamb, served with Roasted Sweet Potatoes, Parsnips and Chickpeas

500ml yoghurt

4tbsp tomato purée

5tbsp olive oil

10 cloves of garlic, finely
chopped

2 dry bay leaves, crumbled

2 sprigs of fresh thyme leaves

1tsp sugar

Salt and pepper

3kg shoulder of lamb, boned
but not rolled

Bunch of fresh mint or coriander,
or a mixture of both would
be lovely

Beat yoghurt with the tomato purée. Still beating, dribble in the olive oil and stir in the garlic, bay leaves, thyme, sugar, salt and pepper.

Make deep incisions all over the shoulder of lamb and pour the marinade over it. Cover and leave in the fridge for 12 hours.

Day of cooking: heat the oven to 200°/Gas 6.

Take the lamb out of the marinade, place it in a roasting tin and put in the oven for one and a half to two hours.

Cover with tin foil for the first hour.

Do check that the pan is not too dry and add a cup of water if needed half an hour before the end of cooking time.

Prepare and cook the vegetables (see recipe page 96).

Take the lamb from the oven, remove to a plate and keep warm.

Put the roasting tray on the hob over a medium heat. Scrape the pan well to loosen all the sticky bits, add two cups of water and reduce the juices to make a nice thick sauce.

Add the chopped herbs if you have them. Sometimes I add a couple of spoons of natural yoghurt and a good squeeze of lemon or lime juice.

Slice the lamb and lay it on a serving plate surrounded with the roast vegetables.

Notes

You could use leg of lamb instead but it is more expensive and the shoulder tastes better.

If you forget to marinate the night before, do it on the day but try and give it at least five hours and don't store it in the fridge.

Roast Sweet Potatoes, Parsnips and Chickpeas

2kg of mixed sweet potatoes
    and parsnips
Olive oil
Salt and pepper
1 x 400g tin chickpeas

A large mixing bowl
A flat roasting tray

Put a roasting tray in the oven to heat.

Peel and chop up vegetables to around the same size, somewhere between 2 and 3cm.

As you chop the vegetables throw them into a large mixing bowl and pour in a couple of good shots of olive oil and season well with salt and pepper.

Mix well with your hands, making sure you have coated all the vegetables with oil. Add more if you really need it (you do not want any excess).

Take your very hot tray from the oven and pour on the vegetables, spreading them out so too many don't overlap.

Roast for about 25 to 30 minutes or until the vegetables are soft when you test them with a knife.

Drain the tin of chickpeas and mix with the roasted vegetables and return to the oven for five minutes to heat through.

Serve in a bowl or leave on the tray to reheat later.

Planning ahead

Defrost 500ml fish stock.
Defrost fish if in freezer.

Spicy Fish Stew with Rice, served with Braised Peas

750g of haddock or pollock,
    or a mixture of both
1 dried or fresh chilli, to taste
Juice of 1 lemon
Salt and pepper
A handful of chopped herbs
    such as parsley, dill, fennel
    and coriander, or a mixture
    if you have them to hand

1 recipe of rice (page 29)
½ recipe of tomato sauce
    (page 44)
500ml fish stock (page 49)

Heat up the tomato sauce over a medium heat and add the fish stock.

Chop the dried chilli finely, add it to the stew and let it simmer for about 15 minutes.

Taste and season if you think it needs it.

Skin, bone and chop up the fish into bite-sized pieces and add to the stew along with the lemon juice.

Mix the fish in well and turn off the heat.

Put the lid on and let it stand for about five minutes.

Remove the lid and sprinkle with the chopped herbs.

Serve with rice.

Notes

Do not reheat once you have added the fish.
To posh up, use less stock and add wine.
Add some saffron.
Use a mixture of shellfish and fish.
Serve with grated Parmesan.

Braised Green Peas

50ml (3tbsp) olive oil
750g frozen peas
Salt

Warm a heavy-based casserole (with a lid).

Add the olive oil and tip in the peas.

Toss well in the oil and season with salt.

Turn the heat to low, place the lid on top and leave the peas to braise for about 15 minutes.

Spanish Vegetable Dish

Another recipe from Rebeca, our Spanish chef. Something so simple can taste so good. The quality and taste of the olive oil is what makes this dish, along with good salt. You can make this dish from what is lying in the bottom of your fridge. I am giving you my winter combination.

6 large potatoes

1 onion, sliced

4 medium carrots

1 small cauliflower

1 parsnip

2 big handfuls of frozen green beans (optional)

Sea salt

Olive oil

Put a large saucepan of water on to boil.

Peel the potatoes, cut into large chunks and add with the sliced onions to the boiling water. Meanwhile, peel and slice the carrots and parsnips thickly, and break up the cauliflower into florets. Add the carrots and parsnips to the saucepan after about eight minutes or when the potato is nearly cooked. Cook for another two minutes.

Finally add the frozen green beans, bring back to the boil and simmer for another minute.

Drain the vegetables, keeping the vegetable water for another dish.

Serve with coarse sea salt (Maldon is the best) and the best olive oil you have.

Notes

The reserved vegetable stock can be used to make the risotto later in the week.

What really makes this dish is the salt and olive oil, so get the best you can.

I cook this dish throughout the year, using whatever is in season. Remember to cook the longest-cooking vegetables first.

Some sliced cold meats go well with this and this keeps the meat eaters happy.

Pork Loin Chops with Durrus Cheese and Marsala, served with Boiled Potatoes and Cabbage

4 boneless loin pork chops

100g smoked streaky bacon, chopped small

A little olive oil

1 onion, finely chopped

8 medium flat brown mushrooms, finely diced

6tbsp Marsala or red wine (150ml)

250g Durrus cheese, diced small

3tbsp chopped parsley

1 recipe of mashed potatoes (from Stage 2 if in the fridge)

1 recipe of boiled cabbage

Put the potatoes on to boil and boil the kettle.

Take a frying pan that is suitable to go under the grill. Warm the pan on a medium heat, add a little olive oil and cook the chopped bacon.

Fry over a medium heat until the fat runs and the bacon turns golden at the edges.

Add the onion and cook over a medium heat for a couple of minutes. Add the mushrooms and a drizzle of oil if there isn't enough fat left from the bacon. Cook until the mushrooms are tender. Turn up the heat a little and then add the Marsala. It will sizzle and spit. With a wooden spatula, scrape up the sediment in the pan and stir into the mixture.

Remove from the heat and spoon the mushrooms, bacon and onions into a small bowl.

Add the cheese and half the parsley, season lightly and mix gently.

Set aside and get the grill hot. Chop the cabbage. Put it in a saucepan, pour enough boiling water to cover and boil for four or five minutes or until just soft. Drain and mix with a little olive oil.

Place the pan back over the heat and, when hot, add a tablespoon of oil. Season the chops and add to the pan, cook for about three minutes and then turn and cook the other side. Whatever you do, don't overcook them or they will dry out. Turn off the heat and spoon the mushroom and cheese mixture over the pork.

Place the pan under the grill for about two minutes, until the cheese is bubbling and the mixture sizzling. Sprinkle over the rest of the parsley and serve.

Notes

Durrus cheese is an unpasteurised cow's cheese made outside the village of Durrus in West Cork. We use it on a pizza with spinach at the Good Things Café.

Any nice strong-tasting semi-soft cheese would be good if you cannot get Durrus.

If you do not eat cheese as a course or for lunch, put any bits in the freezer and use later for cooking.

Lemon and Pinenut Risotto

Olive oil

1 medium onion, finely chopped

300g risotto rice

Zest of 1 large lemon,
   very finely chopped

Salt and pepper

Juice of the lemon

1 litre of chicken, vegetable
   or fish stock

A small glass of Vermouth
   or white wine

40g toasted pinenuts

A handful of chopped basil
   leaves (alternatively use
   parsley; a little tarragon would
   be nice mixed in as well)

100g grated Parmesan

Jar of pesto

Bring the stock to the boil in a saucepan, lower the heat and let simmer.

Warm a heavy-based saucepan and when warm add the oil followed by the onions and lemon zest, season well with salt and pepper, mix well and cook gently for at least 10 minutes with a lid on. The onions need to release their juices and taste sweet.

Add the rice to the onions, coat well in the oil and continue to cook over moderate heat for five minutes without allowing it to colour.

Add the lemon juice and cook for a minute and then add two ladles of stock, stirring all the time so none of the rice sticks to the bottom.

Lower the heat and continue to cook, adding a few ladles of stock each time the rice almost dries out. You need to start tasting after about 15 minutes to check the doneness of the rice. It should only take about 20 minutes from when you started adding the liquid.

Stir in the wine or Vermouth and cook for a minute and then stir in the chopped basil, pinenuts and half of the cheese. Serve with some pesto on top and a good dash of olive oil.

Planning ahead

Make the braised beef for tomorrow night.

Braised Beef with Mashed Potatoes and Carrots

A classic from Elizabeth David. We need to cook more food like this.
You will be surprised how simple and good this dish is.

1kg of thickly sliced
    stewing beef
4 large onions
50g butter
Salt and pepper
Bay leaf
Parsley stalks

Dressing
2 cloves of garlic
A handful of parsley leaves
1tbsp of cider vinegar
4tbsp olive oil
4 anchovy fillets
2 dried chillies, chopped.

Preheat the oven to 150°/Gas 2. Take your pot and generously butter the inside.

Slice the onions thinly and put half of them in the bottom of the pot. Lightly season with salt and pepper, lay the beef on top and season again. Cover with the rest of the onions, season again and tuck in a bay leaf and the parsley stalks. Cut a sheet of greaseproof paper to fit the shape of the pot and smear it with butter. Place it over the onions, butter side down, and tuck in the edges to enclose. Cover with the lid. Place the pot over a moderate flame until you hear a definite sizzle, and then put it in the oven. Cook for two to two and a half hours or until you can break the meat with your hands.

If you are cooking this the day before, at this stage let it cool down and store until you need it. Reheat on a low flame or in a low oven and finish off.

Serve with

1 recipe of mashed potatoes
    (page 37 – if in fridge, do
    Stage 2)

5 medium carrots

A large flameproof pot with
    a lid, one that you are happy
    to put on the table!

Boil the kettle.

Put the potatoes on to boil using the water from the kettle
and follow the recipe for mash.

Boil the kettle for the carrots.

Chop the parsley, garlic, anchovies and chillies as finely as
you can and add the vinegar and olive oil; you will end up
with a coarse oily paste.

Remove the pot from the oven, check that the meat is very
tender and then gently stir in the paste, being careful not to
break up the meat. Replace the lid, return the pot to the oven
and turn it off, leaving the flavours to infuse for about 20
minutes in the waning heat.

Pour boiling water over the carrots and cook to your liking.

Serve by placing the pot of beef in the middle of the table.

Week 3

Recipes

Shopping List

Supermarket

1 x 750g frozen spinach
1 x 400ml tin coconut milk

Vegetables & Fruit

3kg potatoes
7 onions
1 garlic bulb
7 carrots
1 celery
3 parsnips
2 sweet potatoes
2 aubergines
Small bunch of rhubarb
  (buy 1kg extra to make
  crumble on page 316)
1 cucumber
1 red pepper
2 lemons
2 x 2cm ginger
3 bunches parsley
Fresh mint – optional
2 limes

1 green cabbage (such as
  Savoy)
1 turnip

Dairy

250g sour cream
250ml milk
500ml natural yoghurt
  (large tub)
Butter, small pack

Fish Shop

4 whole plaice, fins removed
1 large monkfish tail,
  about 1.5kg

Butcher

1.2kg topside of beef
8–12 large sausages
750g stewing lamb, cubed
500g minced beef (if not left
  over – see page 127)

Other Shopping

Weekend Work for Week 3

This week's work list will be a doddle after last weekend.

Firstly heat the oven for the scones and make and bake them. Prepare the potatoes and put them on to boil. In the meantime cook the rice. After your hard work last week you can just take the stock from the freezer.

You could double the potatoes and have some in the fridge for a quick lunch during the week. If you find two nights of rice a little much, try the couscous on page 32.

1 recipe of brown soda scones (page 25)

    – *Keep some for the weekend and freeze the rest once they've cooled.*

1 recipe of mash to the end of Stage 1

    – for sausages and Marsala (page 123).

2 recipes of rice (page 29)

    – for monkfish (page 120).

    – for spiced roast vegetables (page 128).

Spiced roast vegetables (page 128)

IF NOT IN THE FREEZER

1 litre of chicken or vegetable stock (page 52)

    – for beef (page 119).

175ml fish stock (page 49)

    – for monkfish (page 120).

Plaice grilled with Chilli, Garlic and Lime Juice, with Red Pepper and Cucumber, served with Potato Cake and Green Beans

4 whole plaice, about 450g
each, fins cut off at shop
1 fat clove of garlic,
chopped finely
1 fresh chilli or 1 dried chilli,
soaked in boiling water for 5
minutes and chopped finely
Juice of ½ juicy lime
Olive oil, about 100ml altogether
Salt and pepper
½ cucumber
½ red pepper
1 recipe of potato cake (page 39)
or plain boiled for ease
350g frozen green beans, left in
freezer from last week

Decide which potatoes you are going to cook and get
them ready.

If you have the time, start about one hour before you want to
eat and marinate the fish.

Mix the garlic, chilli, lime juice and a little olive oil to make
it into a runny paste and season with salt and pepper.

Make a deep cut down the back of each fish from head to
tail and then a series of diagonal cuts across from this
to the sides. Do this on both sides and coat the whole fish
with the paste, making sure it get into the slashes.

Meantime, chop the cucumber and red pepper as finely as
you can, season and mix with enough olive oil to make
a dressing.

Fifteen minutes before you are ready to eat, heat the grill until
it is very hot, about five minutes. Grill the fish for five minutes
on each side.

Serve with any juices from the grill pan and sprinkle the
cucumber and red pepper on top.

Serve with the potato cut into wedges and boiled green
beans tossed in a little olive oil and seasoned with salt
and pepper.

Notes

A lovely way to cook whole plaice.

Children like plaice, as it is a nice soft sweet fish. My children call it funky fish because of its spots.

If you have some fresh herbs, do add them with the cucumber and red pepper. Parsley, fennel, dill or coriander would work well.

Planning ahead

Defrost chicken or vegetable stock for tomorrow for the beef.

For the week's recipe I am giving you topside, as it is really a one-pot dish with great results. In the section 'A Few More Good Things' I have included rib roast, which is amazing but a little on the expensive side. However, I can easily justify the expense by telling you that you can make a lovely meat sauce with the meat left between the bones (see page 127), have a few lovely sandwiches or a cold plate with some nice mustards and chutneys and make a stock with the bones and turn it into a noodle or lentil dish. The recipe for topside is quick, simple and easier on the pocket. The brisket on page 296 is one of the cheapest cuts and offers some new flavours. The real secret to any of these recipes turning out well is the source of your meat and how long it has been hung!

A Great Way with Topside of Beef

1kg joint of topside of beef, tied
1 litre of vegetable stock
Salt and pepper
250g sour cream
100g horseradish cream
1 lemon, juiced
Olive oil
6–8 potatoes, scrubbed
4 carrots
400g or ½ a head green
     cabbage
Butter
Parsley, chopped
Grainy mustard

Set the oven to its hottest temperature and boil the kettle. Take your deepest saucepan, add the stock and bring to the boil.

Next add the meat and enough boiled water from the kettle just to cover it.

Turn the heat down as low as possible, using a heat diffuser if necessary. Poach the meat for 25 minutes.

In the meantime, blend the sour cream and horseradish in a bowl, season with salt, pepper and a few drops of lemon juice.

Lift the beef out of the stock, pat it dry, then season it all over and place it in a small roasting dish. Roast for 25 minutes, rest for 15 minutes.

Soon after putting the beef into the oven, bring the stock back to the boil. Add the potatoes and turnips and simmer for about 20 minutes, adding the carrots and cabbage five minutes before the end.

Drain the vegetables, keeping the stock, and toss them in a bowl with the butter.

Thinly slice the beef and serve on top of the vegetables, with a bowl of sour cream sauce spooned over, accompanied by mustard and a jug of stock.

Planning ahead
Keep leftover cooked beef for the meat sauce on page 127.

Monkfish with Saffron, Honey and Vinegar

Based on a Claudia Roden recipe from her cookbook Arabesque. *I prefer to cook the monkfish on the bone. It cooks evenly and looks lovely.*

Olive oil

Salt and pepper

1 large monkfish tail on the
    bone, about 1.5kg, skinned
    and with the grey skin
    removed

1 large onion, finely sliced

½tsp ground cinnamon

1 medium red chilli, deseeded
    and finely chopped

175ml fish stock

½tsp saffron threads, steeped
    in 30ml hot water

4tbsp cider vinegar

4tbsp runny honey, a little less if
    very sweet

75g raisins, soaked in hot water
    for 20 minutes

A big handful of coriander or
    parsley, roughly chopped

Sprinkle of toasted pinenuts

1 recipe of rice (page 29)

Put the kettle on to boil and cook the rice.

Heat a frying pan that is large enough to take the whole tail. Lightly oil the fish and season well with salt and pepper. When the pan is very hot add the oiled fish (to the dry pan) and quickly sear it on each side until it's golden. You just want to colour the outside, not cook the fish through. Remove the fish to a plate.

In the same pan, add a drop of oil and cook the onions until just beginning to turn golden.

Add the cinnamon and chilli and cook for another couple of minutes. Pour on the stock and add the saffron, vinegar and honey. Drain the raisins and add those too. Bring to the boil, then turn down and simmer for about 10 minutes.

Put the fish into the sauce spooning some of the juices over it. Cover the pan with a lid or foil and cook on a very low heat for 10 minutes, or until the fish is cooked through, checking that the thickest part is cooked. Serve with the coriander or parsley and pinenuts sprinkled on top.

Reheat the rice by quickly stirfrying it in a medium hot pan with a drop of olive oil.

Notes

If you cannot get monkfish on the bone, use fillets but remember to cook it less.
It is so important to have all the skin removed from the fish.
It should be a nice clean white without any grey.

Leave out the saffron and use haddock or pollock to make a
less expensive dish; just cook the fish for half the time.
Some honeys are very sweet, so do add the honey to taste.
If you are not a fan of cinnamon, do not be put off this dish,
though a small amount adds a lovely warmth to it.
When I don't get to the fish shop early enough to get monkfish
on the bone, I use the fillet and cook it for less time

Sausages cooked with Juniper and Marsala, served with Mashed Potatoes and Roast Cabbage with Garlic

A real comforting winter dish, taken from Nigel Slater's Appetite *cookbook. Buy the best sausages you can find. I always use some local Gubbeen herby sausages, big and fat and full of meat and flavour.*

50g butter

8–12 sausages, large

4 medium onions, halved and
    sliced thinly

10 juniper berries and bay leaves

1–2tbsp cornflour or plain
    flour, mixed with
    2tbsp water

200ml Marsala or red wine

250ml chicken stock

1tbsp plain Dijon mustard

1 recipe of mashed potatoes,
    (page 37–8)

1 recipe of roast cabbage
    (page 124)

Melt the butter in a heavy-based pan or frying pan set over a moderate heat and add the sausages.

Let them colour lightly, turning them now and again.

Remove the sausages from the pan and add the onions.

Let them cook slowly in the butter and sausage fat, until they are soft and deep gold. They should be be soft enough to squash between your fingers; this will take about 20 minutes.

Set the oven at 180°C/Gas 4. Start the recipe for mashed potatoes.

Lightly crush the juniper berries between your fingers and add to the onions along with the bay leaves.

Turn up the heat to brown the onions. Sprinkle in the cornflour or flour if using. Let it cook for a minute or so, moving the onions round the pan so they do not burn.

Pour in the Marsala and stock and a little salt and pepper and Dijon mustard.

Return the sausages to the gravy and place in the oven. They are ready when they are cooked right through and the gravy is thick, glossy and bubbling.

Serve with mashed potatoes and roast cabbage.

This sauce goes really well with pan-fried lambs liver, served with a slice of grilled streaky bacon.

Roast Cabbage with Garlic

½ head green cabbage,
    such as Savoy
2 cloves of garlic
Olive oil
Salt and pepper
100ml water

Preheat the oven to 200°C/Gas 6.

Cut the cabbage into four wedges, depending on its size.

Put in a bowl with enough oil to evenly coat it and season with salt and pepper.

Chop the garlic finely and rub into the cabbage.

Heat a frying pan and add the cabbage, cut side down, and cook over a medium heat until golden, turning as it cooks.

Add the water to the pan, cover with some parchment or foil and roast in the oven for 15 minutes or until cooked.

Planning ahead

Defrost cooked pork for tomorrow.

Made with Organic Eggs

Meat Sauce

Olive oil

1 large onion, finely chopped

2 celery sticks, finely chopped

2 medium carrots, finely chopped

Salt and pepper

About 6 parsley stalks, finely
    chopped

2 bay leaves

500g cooked beef (or beef and
    pork mixed), minced or finely
    chopped, or 500g fresh
    mince beef

A small cup of milk (optional)

1 x 400g tin tomatoes

3 cloves of garlic, chopped

Parsley leaves

To serve

Pasta of your choice

Heat a saucepan (that has a tight-fitting lid) and add the oil
along with the onions, celery, carrots, parsley stalks and
bay leaves.

Season well with salt and pepper. Give it all a good mix,
making sure to coat the vegetables with the oil, and cook
on a medium heat for about five minutes or until the
vegetables start to soften.

Add the chopped meat and stir for one minute.

Then add the milk and let it boil for a few minutes until the
milk has cooked into the meat. Add the tomatoes and garlic.
Put the sauce to cook on the lowest heat possible and let it
simmer for at least 30 minutes.

Notes

You can add a glass of red or white wine but I prefer to drink it.
*Leave out the milk if you don't use dairy, but it does make the
sauce nice and rich!*
*Use the sauce to go with pasta or to make a pie topped
with spinach and potato.*
*Posh it up....... Add 50g of dried wild mushrooms – eg. porcini
or ceps – pour over some boiling water, leave to soak for
10 minutes and add with the tomatoes.*
*You could use tomato sauce from the freezer and add the
chopped meat, milk and some extra garlic.*

Planning ahead

Defrost a bag of spinach.

Spiced Roast Vegetables with Chickpeas, Spinach and Coconut Milk, served with Rice

This is a dish I made when I needed to fill the freezer of a vegetarian friend. I did not want to go to the shops, so I worked with what I had and the result was a big hit.

½ small turnip

3 parsnips

3 carrots

3 celery sticks

2 medium sweet potatoes

4 fat cloves of garlic

1 dried red chilli, soaked in
    boiling water for 1 minute

2 thumbs of ginger, peeled
    and grated

Olive oil

1 x 400g tinned chickpeas

1 x 750g bag of frozen spinach

1 x 400ml tin coconut milk

1 recipe of rice (page 29)

Heat your oven to its hottest, 250°C/Gas 9, and heat a flat roasting tray (or two if needed).

Peel and chop all the vegetables; bite-sized would be ideal. Put into a big mixing bowl.

Chop the garlic and chilli finely and mix with the grated ginger. Add some salt and pepper and a good shot of olive oil to make a runny sauce, pour over the vegetables and mix with your hands, making sure it is mixed very well.

Take your very hot tray from the oven and spread out the vegetables as evenly as possible. Return to the oven and roast for about 20 minutes or until just cooked.

In the meantime, if the spinach is still frozen, defrost in a saucepan with the lid on over a medium heat. Then drain away as much water as you can.

Drain the tin of chickpeas. Mix the roasted vegetables, drained spinach, chickpeas and coconut milk together in a saucepan. Bring to the boil and simmer for 15 minutes.

Notes
Sometimes I grind up a mixture of cumin, coriander, fennel and cardamom and add to the vegetables when I am roasting them. This works great if you cannot get your hands on fresh ginger. In the summer use peppers, tomatoes, etc. A mixture of summer vegetables would be nice as well. A great way to use up odd vegetables that are hanging around in the fridge. Freezes very well.

Planning ahead
Make the lamb and aubergine stew for tomorrow night.

Spiced Lamb and Aubergine Stew, served with Rice and a Raw Rhubarb, Cucumber and Mint Salad

You will love this dish. It is always a hit at cookery classes.

750g stewing lamb

4–5tsp cumin seeds, or ground

Salt and pepper

Olive oil

1 large onion, chopped

½tsp chilli powder (optional)

2 aubergines, cubed

1 x 400g tin tomatoes

3 cloves of garlic

Natural yoghurt to serve

1 recipe of raw rhubarb and cucumber salad (page 132)

1 recipe of rice (page 29)

Turn the lamb into a bowl. Add enough oil to coat evenly. Mix the cumin together with some salt and pepper and dust over the lamb.

Get a frying pan very hot and brown the lamb on all sides; this will have to be done in batches, as you do not want the meat to stew. As you brown the meat, put it into the saucepan.

Next in the same frying pan cook the onions until soft and add the chilli powder, if using. Cook for a moment and add to the meat.

Then again in the same pan cook the aubergines with a lid on for about 10 minutes until soft or you could do them quickly on a high heat. Add to the meat along with the tomatoes and garlic.

Cover and let it simmer for about 45 minutes to one hour, until meat is tender.

If making in advance, cool and store in the fridge. Reheat on a medium heat.

Meanwhile, cook the rice and prepare the salad.

Reheat the rice by heating a frying pan or wok, adding a drop of oil and stirfrying until very hot.

Serve the lamb with rice, a pot of natural yoghurt and cucumber, rhubarb and mint salad.

Notes

Leave out the lamb and double the aubergines if you want a vegetarian stew.

Make double and freeze half for later.

Make it as spicy as you want!!!

Raw Rhubarb, Cucumber and Mint Salad

Do try this salad when rhubard is in season, from January to May.

4 rhubarb stalks
½ cucumber
2tbsp coarse salt
1tbsp lemon juice
Chopped mint leaves
Olive oil

Chop rhubarb and cucumber thinly, toss with the coarse salt and let stand for 10 minutes; rinse and drain.
In a bowl, mix the rhubarb and cucumber with lemon juice, adding enough for a slight mouth-tingling effect. Scatter the mint leaves and a good splash of oil on top and serve.

Week 4

Recipes

Shopping List

Supermarket

450g frozen peas
750g frozen spinach
50g dried wild mushrooms
  (or 500g fresh)

Vegetables & Fruit

8kg potatoes
13 onions
3 garlic bulbs
4 carrots
1 celery (if not in fridge)
1 head cabbage (Savoy)
450g brussel sprouts
  (or head of cabbage)
500g chestnut mushrooms
  (if not using dried)
4 tomatoes
1 lemon (for juice)
1 organic lemon

2 x 2cm ginger
2 oranges
1 bunch of spring onions
  (optional)
2 limes
2 bunches of parsley
  (or 1 bunch of coriander
  and 1 bunch of parsley)

Dairy

200ml double cream
50g Parmesan

Fish Shop

4 x 250g hake or
  two large fillets
800g haddock, skinned
  and boned

Butcher

1 chicken (2kg)
4 pork loin chops
1kg stewing beef
150g unsmoked streaky bacon
200g pork skin

Other Shopping

Weekend Work for Week 4

There are a lot of potatoes to prepare this weekend, so you need to ask somebody round for a chat! Otherwise your list is rather short.

As you have a short list and it would be nice to have a change from the brown scones, why not give the white yeast bread on page 26 a go.

You might find three nights of mash too much, so you could make rice to go with the meat stew on page 154.

1 recipe of brown soda scones (page 25)
- – cooled and frozen.
- – *Keep some back for the weekend.*

3 recipes of mash to the end of Stage 1 (page 37)
- – for fish pie (page 144).
- – for pork with prunes (page 147).
- – for Provençal meat and wine stew (page 154).

IF NOT IN THE FREEZER FROM WEEK 2
1 recipe of tomato sauce (page 44)
- – for fish pie (page 144).
- – *Freeze the rest for later.*

Roast Fish on a Bed of Onions and Thyme, served with Mashed Potatoes and Peas

This recipe will take a little more time in the kitchen due to the cooking of the onions, but you can do double and make the onion and cider soup on page 262. Also lovely to top a pizza.

1kg onions
Olive oil
A few sprigs of thyme
2 bay leaves
4 x 250g thick fillets of hake
   or two large fillets
Salt and pepper

1 recipe of peas (page 99)
Boiled potatoes

Heavy-based saucepan
Shallow roasting tray

Slice the onions as thinly as you can while you heat the saucepan over a medium heat.

Add enough olive oil to coat the bottom of the pan and add the onions, giving them a good mix. Season well and add the thyme and bay leaves. Cook for about five minutes.

Continue to cook on a low heat with a lid on for about 40 minutes or until the onions are very soft and almost purée-like. Twenty minutes before eating, heat the oven to its hottest. Boil the kettle and cook the potatoes.

Lightly oil an oven tray and spread out the onion mixture evenly on it. Season the fish and lay it on top of the bed of onions. Bake in the preheated oven for about eight to 10 minutes or until the fish is cooked. Test the thickest part by pressing with your fingers – fish should be soft to touch when cooked.

In the meantime, cook the peas.

Roast Chicken, served with Roast Potatoes and Sprouts stirfried with Ginger and Orange

I could eat roast chicken every week. When it's good it's very good.

1 chicken (2kg) – the best you can buy

Olive oil

1 lemon – should be organic or the gravy will taste bitter

Some fresh hard herbs – rosemary, thyme and bay

1 head of garlic, cut in half across

2 large onions, chopped with the skin on

2 celery sticks, roughly chopped

2 carrots, roughly chopped

1 recipe roast potatoes (page 43)

1 recipe of sprouts (page 143)

Take a roasting tin or oven-proof frying pan with sides no deeper than 5cm.

Set the oven at 250°C/Gas 9, placing a rack towards the top.

Open up the chicken, removing any strings, and rub it all over with oil, even putting a little inside the bird.

Season the bird all over with salt and pepper. Cut the lemon in two, put one half inside and squeeze the other over the chicken.

Lay the chopped onion, celery, carrot and garlic in the middle of the tin, season with salt and pepper. Lay the chicken, breast side down, on top.

Roast for one hour, turning the heat down to 200°C/Gas 7 if the chicken is starting to burn on top. This is more likely with a fan oven, so keep an eye on it.

After half an hour into the cooking time, boil the potatoes for roasting. Prepare the vegetables and cook while the gravy is simmering.

Turn the bird the right way up on an oven-proof plate and return to the oven to brown the skin. This should take about 15 minutes. Now you can make the gravy.

The chicken is ready when the juices run clear when the flesh is deeply pierced with a skewer. Remove it from the oven and let it rest for a few minutes.

Notes

Keep leftover chicken for night five for chicken in coconut milk with spices.

oods Ltd.

Irish

Range

Chicken

(Class A)

O: BMC-A2 H.A.C.C.P. APPROVED

Sprouts with Ginger and Orange

Olive oil

1 small onion, finely chopped

1 thumb of root ginger,
    peeled and grated

450g Brussels sprouts,
    trimmed and halved

Juice and zest of 1 very
    juicy orange

Salt, pepper and a pinch of
    brown sugar

A few gratings of nutmeg

Heat a frying pan or wok to medium heat and add a good splash of oil.

Add the onion, ginger, orange zest, salt and pepper.

Cook until the onions are soft but not brown. Covering with a lid helps to soften the onions.

Add the sprouts and raise the heat. Stirfry for a couple of minutes, add the orange juice and mix in well or until the juice has almost evaporated.

Add a sprinkle of sugar, taste and season with salt and pepper if needed

Notes

When sprouts are not in season, make the above recipe with cabbage. You can use the half head of cabbage left from last week.

Fish Pie, served with Peas cooked in Olive Oil

800g of haddock, skinned, with
    the pinhead bones removed
750g frozen spinach, defrosted
    or frozen
Salt and pepper
Lemon
1 recipe of mashed potatoes
    (page 37)
Olive oil

½ recipe of tomato sauce
    (page 44)
500ml fish stock (page 49)
1 recipe of braised peas
    (page 99)

A saucepan that can go from hob to oven to table is ideal here and will save a lot of washing up.

Heat the oven to 220°/Gas 7.

Heat the tomato sauce in the saucepan and add the fish stock. When it all comes to the boil, let it simmer for a few minutes to reduce a little.

Meanwhile, if you did not take out the spinach to defrost, defrost it in a saucepan with a lid on a low heat; this should take about five minutes. Drain through a sieve, getting rid of as much water as you can, and give it a good squeeze.

Season with salt and pepper and a squeeze of lemon juice.

Chop up the fish into bite-sized pieces.

Take the tomato sauce off the heat and add the fish.

Spread the spinach on top of the fish mixture, followed by the mashed potato. Drizzle well with olive oil and bake in the oven for 20 minutes or until everything is bubbling and the potato is just a little brown at the edge.

Place the pie in the middle of the table and serve with the peas.

Notes

To posh it up…
Use a mixture of fish and shellfish.
Add some saffron and a splash of wine.

Pork with Prunes, served with Mashed Potato and stirfried Cabbage with Garlic and Juniper

This is one of my favourite dishes from Jane Grigson's Good Things *and a favourite staff treat at the café – although not really a dish to have before an evening's work; more suited to an evening in front of the fire in the winter. A pork chop has never tasted so good.*

12 large prunes

Glass of white wine

4 pork loin chops

Knob of butter

Salt and pepper

1tsp redcurrant jelly

200ml double cream

1 recipe of mashed potato (page 37), or boiled potatoes

1 recipe of stirfried cabbage (page 149)

A small saucepan

A large frying pan

Boil the kettle.

Put the potatoes on to boil, if you don't have mash already in the fridge.

Place the prunes in a bowl and pour over enough boiling water to cover. Leave to soak until the water goes cold, then drain.

Put the prunes along with the wine into a small saucepan, bring to the boil and let simmer on a very low heat until the prunes are nice and soft, about 30 minutes.

Heat the frying pan and melt the butter.

Season the chops with salt and pepper and cook on both sides until the juices run clear, turning the heat down after you have browned both sides so the chops will cook through and not burn on the outside. If you have a lid that will cover the chops in the pan, it will help them to cook evenly.

In the meantime, prepare and cook the cabbage.

Remove the chops from the pan to a warm plate, add the wine and prunes to the pan along with the redcurrant jelly and cream.

Bring everything to the boil and let it simmer for a couple of minutes to cook the cream and bring the flavours together. Pour over the pork and serve with mashed potato and cabbage.

Notes

A pork fillet or pork steak would be a lovely cut here, but do not overcook it or it will become dry.

Stirfried Cabbage with Garlic and Juniper

1 head of Savoy cabbage or a
    nice green head, quartered
    and sliced
Olive oil
4 cloves of garlic, finely chopped
4 to 6 juniper berries, crushed
    between your fingers
Salt and pepper
Small cup of water

Heat a frying pan or wok to a medium heat and add a splash of oil. Add the cabbage and stirfry for a couple of minutes on a high heat, then add the juniper berries and cook for another minute.

Lower the heat, add the garlic and mix in well. Season with salt and pepper.

Add a small cup of water, turn up the heat and cook until the water has evaporated and the cabbage is cooked to your liking.

Coconut Chicken with Spices and Herbs

1tsp cumin seeds

1tsp coriander seeds

4 cardamom pods (optional)

1 large onion, finely chopped

1 celery stick, finely chopped

Thumb size of grated ginger

4 cloves of garlic

2 limes – one for zest and juice,
   the other for serving

1 chilli, finely chopped, or use a
   dried chilli that has been
   soaked in boiling water

A big bunch of coriander
   (or parsley); separate the
   stalks from the leaves and
   chop the stalks finely

Salt and pepper

400ml tin of coconut milk

Coriander or parsley leaves,
   lightly chopped

400g (or as near as possible)
   chicken picked from the
   leftover roast chicken

1 bunch of spring onions,
   finely chopped (optional)

1 recipe of rice (page 29)

Wok, saucepan, or
   big frying pan

Heat the wok and toast the cumin, coriander and cardamom for a couple of minutes.

Next add a little oil to the toasted spices and add the onions, celery, ginger, lime zest, chilli and herb stalks, season with salt and pepper and soften over a low heat for about five minutes. You might need a little more oil but make sure you do not brown the vegetables

Add the coconut milk, bring to the boil and let it simmer for a few minutes.

Finally add the chicken and let it warm through without letting it boil.

Add the lime juice and sprinkle the top with the chopped coriander leaves and spring onions.

Reheat the rice by heating a pan to very hot and adding a drop of oil to coat the bottom. Stirfry the rice until very hot. Serve with segments of lime.

Notes

This is a great way to use up bits of odd vegetables that are hanging around in your fridge.

To bulk it out, add a bag of frozen spinach (defrosted) towards the end or serve spinach separately with a good squeeze of lemon juice.

If you get to shop at an Asian supermarket, you can buy lots of nice things to add to this dish. Lime leaves, lemon grass, Thai fish sauce, shrimp paste and big bunches of fresh herbs.

To make it vegetarian

Roast a mixture of vegetables and add instead of the chicken.

Mushroom Risotto

500g flat or chestnut mushrooms
  (or 50g dried wild
  mushrooms)
1 onion, peeled and finely
  chopped
Olive oil
Salt and pepper
1 litre chicken or vegetable
  stock (or the soaking water
  topped up with stock)
300g arborio rice
50g butter (optional)
Half-glass Vermouth or
  white wine
40g to 50g Parmesan or
Desmond cheese, add to taste

Heat a heavy-based saucepan and add the oil then the onions. Season well with salt and pepper and cook gently for at least 10 minutes with a lid on until the onion is soft. The onions need to release their juices and taste sweet. Add the mushroom to the onions, turning up the heat, and cook for two minutes.

Heat the stock in a separate saucepan until it is boiling, then lower the heat and allow it to simmer.

Stir the rice into the onions and mushrooms and coat it in the oil, continuing to cook over a moderate heat for five minutes without allowing it to colour.

Add two ladles of stock to the rice, stirring all the time so none of the rice sticks to the bottom.

Lower the heat and continue to cook, adding a few ladles of stock each time the rice almost dries out. Continue until the rice is cooked. You need to start tasting after about 15 minutes to check if the rice is done. If you run out of stock, use boiling water.

When the rice is cooked, stir in the butter, if using, Vermouth and grated cheese.

If using dried mushrooms, soak them in boiling water for 15 minutes. Chop and add to the rice with the first ladle of stock. Use the soaking water as stock and finish off with stock.

Notes
Other winter risotto ideas:
Squash – peel, deseed and dice and add when the onions are soft.
Fennel and pea – quarter and slice the fennel thinly and soften with the onions. Boil a pack of frozen peas and add at the end of the cooking time. A dash of Pernod would be lovely here. Great with some pan-fried fish.

Planning ahead
Make the dish for tomorrow night (page 154).

153

Provençal Meat and Wine Stew served with Mashed Potato

Olive oil

1kg stewing beef

150g unsmoked streaky bacon

200g fresh pork skin with
excess fat removed

2 onions, chopped

2 carrots, chopped

4 fresh tomatoes, chopped

2 cloves of garlic, peeled and
flattened (not chopped)

A bunch made of thyme, bay
leaf, parsley, tied together
with string (not coloured)

Zest of ½ an orange

Glass of red wine

Salt and pepper

**Dressing for the finished dish
(optional)**

2 cloves of garlic

medium bunch of parsley

Zest of ½ an orange

1 recipe of mashed potato
(page 37)

In the bottom of the pot put the olive oil, then the bacon and the vegetables. Arrange the meat on top, season well with salt and pepper. Sprinkle on the orange zest.

Bury the garlic cloves and the bunch of herbs in the centre of the meat. Cover with the pork skin, fat side down.

With the pan uncovered, start the cooking on a moderate heat on top of the stove.

After about 10 minutes, put the wine into another saucepan and bring it to a fast boil, then pour the bubbling wine over the meat. Cover the pot with greaseproof paper and place the lid on top. Transfer to a very slow oven and leave for two and a half hours. Remove the paper and the pork skin from the top.

It is now ready to serve.

If you are cooking in advance, leave the paper and skin on top and cool down. Reheat when needed and remove the paper and skin.

Make the mashed potatoes.

At the serving stage, chop the garlic, parsley and orange zest together and sprinkle over the top.

Serve with a green salad dressed with olive oil and Maldon salt and a splash of cider vinegar.

Summer

Week 5

Recipes

Shopping List

Supermarket

3 x 400g tins tomatoes

Vegetables & Fruit
5.2kg potatoes
8 onions
3 carrots
1 celery
1 cucumber
3 red peppers
6 tomatoes
3 garlic bulbs
1.5 aubergines
3 lemons
2 limes (if not using lemon)
1 packet chillies (6–8 chillies
    will keep in the fridge for a
    month)
250g eating apples
250g pears
2 ripe bananas
3 bunches parsley
1 bunch mint (optional)

Salad leaves for 8 people
2 courgettes
2 red onions

Dairy
250ml natural yoghurt
1 dozen eggs

Fish Shop

4 medium whole fish or
    4 x 250g fillets
700g haddock or pollock,
    skinned and boned

Butcher

3–4kg shoulder of lamb
    on the bone
8–10 big sausages
250g streaky bacon
1kg shin beef, cubed
    (or sliced)

A piece of pork skin or
    a pig trotter

Other Shopping

Weekend Work for Week 5

This is the first work list of the summer weeks and the list – like the food – has got lighter. Begin by heating the oven and bake the scones. Next prepare the tomato sauce and while it is simmering peel and boil the potatoes. In the meantime put the rice on to boil. By now the potatoes should be ready to mash. Allow everything to cool down while you tidy up and get the evening meal ready.

1 recipe of brown soda scones (page 25)
- *Cool and freeze them, keeping some back for tomorrow.*

1 recipe of mashed potatoes to the end of Stage 1
- for fish cakes, 500g (page 170).
- for beef stew (page 178).

1 recipe of tomato sauce (page 44)
- for stolen Cuban dish (page 174).
- *The rest to go into the freezer for Week 6.*

2 recipes of rice (page 29)
- for stolen Cuban dish (page 174).
- for aubergines stewed with tomatoes and spices (page 177).

Baked Fish with Oven Potatoes and a Dressing of Rosemary, Anchovy and Capers

4 medium whole fish or
    4 x 250g fish fillets
500g potatoes, peeled or
    unpeeled
Salt and pepper
Olive oil
4 medium sprigs of rosemary
Small dried red chilli (only if
    you want a bit of heat!)
2 fat cloves of garlic
2 anchovy fillets
4 large sprigs of parsley
About 8–12 capers
Juice of 1 small lemon

To serve
Salad leaves for 4
Olive oil
Maldon salt

A pan or tray that can go on
the hob and in the oven

Turn the oven to 225°/Gas 9 and heat an oven tray.
Cut the potatoes into thin slices. Wash under running water
for five minutes and dry. Put into a large mixing
bowl and add a good dash of olive oil, making sure you
have enough to coat all the potatoes. Season well with salt
and pepper.

Take the hot tray from the oven, spread out the potatoes
evenly and return to the oven to bake for about 10 minutes or
until the potatoes are nearly soft in the centre. Do give them
a mix around about halfway through and add a drop more oil
if they are sticking too much.

While the potatoes are baking make the dressing by chopping
the needles of the rosemary, the dried chilli, garlic, anchovies
and parsley (I pile everything together on the chopping
board and chop all in one go). Put it all in a mixing bowl and
add the lemon juice and enough olive oil to make it runny like
a dressing, about three tablespoons

When the potatoes are ready, lay the fish on top of them,
spoon over the dressing and bake for about 15–20 minutes
for whole fish and about 10 minutes for the fillets.

Serve with a green salad dressed with olive oil and a
little salt.

Planning ahead

*Poach the fish for fish cakes (see page 170). Cool down and
keep covered in the fridge until needed.*

Roast Shoulder of Lamb with Roast Vegetables and Potatoes

The shoulder is my all-time favourite cut of lamb; it has great flavour and is always a great price. Cooking on the bone is so much better for flavour. It will not give you neat slices but who will care when it tastes so good. This is home cooking!!!

1 whole shoulder of lamb on the
    bone, about 3 to 4kg
3 large onions, roughly chopped
3 carrots, roughly chopped
3 sticks of celery, roughly
    chopped
4 bay leaves
2 heads of garlic, split in half
1 big bunch of fresh mint or
    1 tablespoon of mint jelly
Redcurrant jelly

1 recipe of roast potatoes
    (page 43)
1 recipe of roast vegetables
    (page 169)
1 recipe of gravy (page 34)

A frying pan or roasting tray
    that can go in the oven and
    on the hob

Set the oven at 250°/Gas 9, placing a rack in the middle. Spread all the chopped vegetables in your roasting tray, along with the bay leaves, garlic and the stalks of the mint (keep the mint leaves for the gravy), and season well with salt and pepper.

Lay the lamb on top, season well with salt and pepper and put in the middle of the hot oven.

After about 45 minutes, when the joint should be nicely browned, turn the oven down to 190°/Gas 5. DO CHECK AFTER ABOUT 30 MINUTES IN CASE YOUR OVEN IS TOO HOT. Continue to cook the meat for another hour and a half. Remove the meat from the roasting tray and allow to rest in a warm place.

Make the gravy and at the end stir in a large tablespoon of redcurrant jelly and the chopped mint leaves or mint sauce. Serve with roast potatoes and roasted vegetables or peas in olive oil with salad.

Notes

After the initial high heat you can lower your oven to 160°/Gas 3 and cook the meat more slowly if this suits your plans on Sunday – lots of papers to read, a long walk or a trip to the cinema and it will not come to any harm.

Stuffings

You can stuff the meat with a mixture of chopped anchovies and garlic, or garlic and rosemary, and add a tin of tomatoes with the water to your gravy and you will have a completely different dish.

Try using some chopped dried seaweed such as Dulse instead of anchovies.

Planning ahead

Keep leftover lamb for the aubergine dish on page 177.

Roast Vegetables

Olive oil

Salt and pepper

4 large ripe tomatoes

2 courgettes

2 medium red onions

2 red peppers

1 aubergine

While the oven is high for the lamb, preheat a shallow roasting tray big enough to take the vegetables.

Prepare all the vegetables – quarter the tomatoes, courgettes, red onions, peppers, slice the aubergines – and put in a mixing bowl. Coat well in olive oil and season with salt and pepper. Remove the very hot tray from the oven and pour on your vegetables, spreading them out. Return to the oven and roast for about 25 minutes (with the lamb) or until the vegetables are soft and a little charred. They can then be removed and reheated in the oven as you make the gravy.

Fish Cakes with Salsa

700g skinless fillets of white
fish, such as haddock or
white pollock, bones removed
750g potatoes, peeled, cooked
and mashed (if not already
done)
A good big bunch of chopped
dill or parsley or a mixture
Salt and pepper
A very good squeeze of
lemon juice
Oatmeal or cornmeal for
dusting
Olive oil for frying

Poach the fish gently in salted water for three or four minutes, drain, allow to cool and then flake the flesh.

Mix together the potato, fish, herbs, lemon juice, salt and pepper until well amalgamated.

Mould the mixture into four large rounds cakes, about 3cm thick, or eight smaller ones and refrigerate for about an hour if you have the time, as they will be easier to cook.

Lightly press the chilled fish cakes in the oatmeal, shaking off any excess, and fry them in the olive oil for about three or four minutes on each side until golden brown.

You can also bake them in a preheated oven, 200°C/Gas 6, on an oiled tray for about 15 minutes, turning halfway through the cooking.

For the salsa

1 small onion (white or red)
  or a bunch of spring onions

½ cucumber

1 small red or yellow pepper

2 tomatoes

1 medium red chilli or one
  dried chilli soaked in boiling
water (optional)

Parsley or coriander

Juice of 1 lemon or 2 limes

Salt and pepper

Olive oil

While the fish cakes are cooking, make the salsa by chopping all the vegetables as finely as you can and mixing them together in a bowl with salt, pepper, lemon juice and olive oil. Taste as you season and stop when you are happy.

Serve with salad leaves simply dressed with olive oil and Maldon salt.

Notes

If you have the time, make double the recipe and freeze half the fish cakes.

I always make extra salsa and keep it for another night to go with a curry or pan-fried fish. Also great for lunch with some hummus and pitta bread.

Tonight is an ideal night for a dessert, try the apple and blackberry crumble on page 316.

Pan-fried Sausages with a Potato, Bacon, Apple, Pear and Thyme Braise

I got the idea of the braise from Diana Henry's lovely book Roast Figs Sugar Snow.

8–10 big sausages
Olive oil
1kg potatoes
250g eating apples
250g pears
Olive oil
250g streaky bacon, cut into
    chunks about 2cm square
Salt and pepper
Nutmeg
2 sprigs fresh thyme
1 bay leaf

Heat the frying pan and add a drop of olive oil, just enough to cover the bottom of the pan. Brown the sausages on all sides over a medium heat.

Turn the heat down to the lowest and, using a heat diffuser, let the sausages cook while you prepare the braise. Remember to turn the sausages the odd time.

Heat a saucepan, add a good splash of oil and cook the bacon on a medium heat for a couple of minutes.

Meanwhile, cut the potatoes in chunks of about 3cm and add to the bacon, giving it a good stir.

Core and slice the apples and pears and add to the pot, giving it a good mix in the juices. Season and add the thyme and bay leaf.

Cover the saucepan and cook over a very low heat for about

20–30 minutes or until everything is nice and soft.
Give the pot a good shake now and again but avoid opening
the lid as you will lose steam – the pears go into a lovely
gooey sweet mush.
Serve with the sausages, which should now be well cooked
and nice and sticky.

Notes
The potato braise goes well with any pork dish.
If you use cooking apples, add some brown sugar; these will
cook into a mush rather quickly.
I sometimes double the recipe, add extra bacon and serve it
with fried or poached eggs.

Stolen Cuban Dish

Please, please do not be put off this dish when you read the ingredients. When Rebeca, our Spanish chef, first made it for us at the café I was not looking forward to it, but I was soon won over. It really works, is so simple and you are using ingredients you already have. It has become a big hit with my cookery students and so many now make it at home.

Olive oil
2 very ripe bananas
4–8 eggs

500g cooked rice (page 29)
½ recipe of tomato sauce (or 1 portion) (page 44)

Cook the rice and the tomato sauce or reheat if you have them already made. Heat a frying pan and add some olive oil, cut the bananas in four lengthways and fry quickly on both sides until nicely brown. Remove from the pan and keep warm on a plate over the rice or sauce.

In the same frying pan add a little more olive oil and fry the eggs to your liking – nice runny eggs work well here.

On a large serving plate layer the dish, starting first with the rice, followed by the tomato sauce and topped with the fried eggs. Finally arrange the bananas around the dish.

Notes
Every student should know about this dish before they leave home. You can use up the unwanted brown bananas at the bottom of the fruit bowl.

Aubergines stewed with Tomatoes and Spices, served with Rice

This aubergine stew will go well with the leftover lamb from Sunday.

1kg aubergines, cubed
1 large onion (about 500g),
    chopped
4 cloves of garlic
1 x 400g tin chopped tomatoes
1tsp cinnamon
1tsp allspice
1tsp cumin
75g raisins
Large bunch of parsley, chopped
½ cucumber
250ml natural yoghurt
A good handful of fresh mint,
    if available

1 recipe of cooked rice
    (page 29)

Warm a medium-sized saucepan and add enough olive oil to just cover the bottom.

Add the chopped onions and cook for about five minutes on a medium heat.

Add a little more oil, turn up the heat, add the aubergines and cook for about five minutes.

Add the tomatoes, garlic, spices, raisins and parsley, give it all a good mix and let it simmer for at least 20 minutes.

Serve warm or at room temperature, sprinkle with some chopped mint and serve with cold slices of lamb, the sliced cucumber and yoghurt.

Reheat the rice by stirfrying it in a very hot pan with a little oil.

Notes
Make double the recipe and freeze some for a later date.
Goes well with couscous.

Planning ahead
Cook tomorrow night's dish.

Beef Stew with Tomatoes and a Topping of Lemon Garlic and Parsley

Served with mashed potatoes and green salad.

2 large onions, finely chopped

Salt and pepper

1kg shin beef, sliced or cubed

A good pinch of oregano

4 large cloves of garlic, chopped

Olive oil

A large piece of pork skin, with not too much fat, or a trotter/ crubeen

150ml red wine

2 x 400g tins tomatoes

1tbsp dark brown sugar

1tbsp tomato concentrate

For the topping

Zest of a lemon, finely chopped

2 cloves of garlic, finely chopped

A big handful of chopped parsley

To serve

1 recipe of mashed potatoes (page 37), or take from the fridge and do Stage 2

Salad leaves for 4

A heavy-based saucepan

Preheat the oven at 150°/Gas 2.

Heat the saucepan and add enough olive oil to coat the bottom. Add the chopped onions and cook over a gentle heat until soft and not too brown.

Season the meat well with salt, pepper and oregano and add to the onions, raise the heat and lightly brown the meat.

Pour in the wine, tomatoes and chopped garlic and bring gently to the boil.

Lay the pork skin on top of the meat with the fat side down (this will keep the dish nice and moist and will stop the meat from drying out) or put the trotter into the middle of the meat. Put the lid on and place in the middle of the oven and cook until the meat is tender, this will take at least three hours.

The dish is now ready to eat and may be served directly from the pot. I do like to remove the meat and reduce the sauce by letting it boil on a high heat, so that the liquid is less, the flavour is more intense and more importantly it will seem that you are serving meat with a sauce; it will look less stew-like.

I like to finely chop the pork skin or trotter and add to the sauce. If making in advance, cool down and keep in the fridge or make the topping and serve.

For the topping mix all the ingredients together and sprinkle on top of the sauce. Don't be mean with the parsley.

Serve with mashed potatoes and a green salad dressed with olive oil.

Notes

I like to make this dish the day before, leaving the meat in the sauce overnight, reheating it about 45 minutes before dinner, removing the meat and reducing the sauce while the potatoes are boiling.

Week 6

Recipes

Shopping List

Supermarket

24 olives with stones in
750g frozen peas

Vegetables & Fruit

2kg Rooster potatoes
2.5kg new potatoes
4 large baking potatoes
10 onions
3 carrots
2 fennel bulbs
20 cherry tomatoes or
　5 regular tomatoes
2 garlic bulbs
6 lemons
1 cucumber
5 heads of salad
1 bunch parsley
1 bunch basil or parsley
1 bunch tarragon
1 small bunch mint
4 large ripe tomatoes

1 celery (if not left over)
Coriander (optional)

Dairy

400g butter
200–250g feta cheese

Fish Shop

4 x 250g John Dory fillets or
　fish of your choice
4 x 250g fish fillets of your
　choice

Butcher

1 chicken (2kg)
4 pork chops on the bone
　with skin on
1kg shoulder of lamb, cubed

Other Shopping

Weekend Work for Week 6

This week's list is very short and you will be in and out of the kitchen in less than half an hour. Take this opportunity to sort out your fridge and make a soup with any of those vegetables lying in the bottom before they make their way to the compost. If you have tried the white bread already, why not give it another go this week. Practice makes perfect.

1 recipe of brown soda scones (page 25)
- *Cool and freeze them, remembering to keep some back for tomorrow or this evening!*

2 recipes of rice (page 29)
- 1 for fish with tomato, caper and herb sauce (page 195).
- 1 for Moroccan lamb (page 204).

Peel 1 kg potatoes, cover with water and keep in the fridge to make potato cake to go with the tasty pork chops on page 196.

FROM THE FREEZER

1 portion of tomato sauce (page 44)
- for fish with tomato, caper and herb sauce (page 195).

200ml of fish stock (page 49)
- for fish with tomato, caper and herb sauce (page 195).

Fish baked with Cherry Tomatoes, Basil and Olives, served with New Potatoes and Green Salad

4 x 250g of firm white fish fillets

About 16 black olives –
   not in brine

1 clove of garlic, finely chopped

1 small dried red chilli,
   finely chopped

1 good handful fresh basil
   or parsley, roughly chopped

3tbsp of olive oil

20 cherry tomatoes, halved, or
   5 tomatoes, halved or
   quartered

Juice of 1 lemon

Salt and pepper

Potatoes for 4

Salad for 4

Maldon salt

Olive oil

Heat the oven at 250°C/Gas 9, heating up a roasting tray big enough to take the fish. Boil the kettle for the potatoes.

Mix all the ingredient except the fish and leave to sit while you wash the potatoes and salad.

Put the potatoes in lightly salted boiling water, set over a high heat and cook for about 15–20 minutes depending on their size. Season the fish with salt and pepper.

Remove the hot roasting tray from the oven (with an oven cloth), spread a little of the liquid from the dressing on the bottom and lay the fish on top. Spread the rest of the dressing over the fish.

Cover the whole roasting tray with foil, sealing it as tightly as you can, and it return to the hot oven.

Bake for about eight minutes, remove from the oven and allow to stand, covered, for a couple of minutes while you drain the potatoes and dress the salad with some olive oil and a good pinch of Maldon salt.

Remove the foil and place in the middle of the table.

Notes

I got this idea from one of Jamie Oliver's books one day when I wanted something quick to make. You can do it in four separate packages but I find it hard to fit them into a small oven without overlapping. I always make extra dressing and use it later in the week with fish cakes or with pan-fried duck breast and green salad leaves. John Dory is my favourite fish for this dish, as it is firm and sweet, but when I am feeling broke I use pollock or thick fillets of haddock. I often use regular tomatoes, because sometimes I cannot let myself buy cherry tomatoes as they are very expensive and I feel I am paying more for the plastic carton.

Roast Chicken with Tarragon Butter, served with New Potatoes and Braised Peas with Lettuce

This week I am giving you two recipes for roast chicken. The shopping list takes in chicken with tarragon butter but do give the Migas a try. Remember to add milk and spring onions to the shopping list.

Chicken (2kg) –
   the best you can buy
A good bunch of Tarragon –
   usually a supermarket pack
   is more than plenty
100g butter, very soft but
   not melted!!!
Salt and pepper
2 large onions, chopped with
   the skin on
2 celery sticks,
   roughly chopped
2 carrots, roughly chopped
Bay leaves

Gravy (page 34)
Braised peas and lettuce
   (page 191)
Potatoes for 4

Roughly chop the tarragon (keep a tablespoon back to sprinkle into the gravy before serving) and put into a bowl along with the butter and a little salt and pepper.
Gently loosen the skin of the chicken away from the breast and leg meat with your hand.
Mix the tarragon and butter together well and push in under the loose skin, making sure you spread it down into the legs. Smooth the skin down, making sure the butter is well spread out underneath.
Lightly rub the chicken all over with a little olive oil and season well with salt and pepper.
Lay the chopped onion, celery and carrots in the middle of the tin and place the chicken breast side down on top.
Roast for 50 minutes, turning the heat down to 200°/Gas 7 if the chicken is starting to burn on top.
Remove the roasting tray from the oven, turn the bird the right way up on an oven-proof plate and return to the oven to brown the skin. This should take about 15 minutes. Now you can make the gravy. Place the roasting tray with the vegetables on a high heat and add enough tap water to cover. Finish the gravy following the recipe on page 34.
In the meantime, boil the kettle and pour over the potatoes with a good pinch of salt and let simmer for about 10 minutes or until cooked.

Cook the peas with lettuce (see recipe page 191).

Slice the tomatoes on to a plate, season with Maldon salt and sprinkle with olive oil.

When you have strained the gravy, add the reserved tarragon and serve with the chicken.

The chicken is ready when the juices run clear when the flesh is deeply pierced with a skewer. Remove it from the oven and let it rest for a few minutes.

Notes

If you want to avoid the butter, chop the tarragon and mix with oil, salt and pepper and use as for butter.

Make a stock as on page 51. Or freeze the bones until you have another chicken carcass.

Braised Green Peas and Lettuce

50ml (3tbsp) olive oil

10–20 firm, crisp lettuce leaves, washed and drained, but not dried

750g frozen green peas

3 sprigs of mint

Salt

Lightly olive oil a heavy-based casserole or saucepan (lid included) into which the peas will fit quite neatly. Tip in the frozen green peas, toss well to coat in the oil and add the mint, pushing it down into the peas. Sprinkle with salt and cover with the lettuce leaves.

Cover the pan tightly and cook over a gentle heat for about 20 minutes, shaking the pan occasionally, holding the lid down firmly as you do.

Stir in the lettuce leaves and serve.

Planning ahead

Defrost tomato sauce if not already in the fridge.

Keep leftover chicken for rice noodles with chicken (page 203).

Chicken with Migas

A very simple way to brighten up a plain roast chicken. This recipe brings a little sunshine to the table. By using up some stale bread along with some store-cupboard items, you are in for a treat.

1.7kg roasting chicken

Salt and pepper

2tbsp balsamic vinegar

2tbsp cider vinegar

200g slightly stale bread, made into rough breadcrumbs

50ml water

50ml milk

75g raisins

Olive oil

4 spring onions, cut into 3cm lengths, or 2 red onions, quartered (optional)

75g pinenuts (optional)

A big head of salad, butterhead is lovely here, or a mixed leaf salad

While the chicken is roasting prepare the migas. Moisten the bread with the water and milk and let it sit for about an hour. Put the raisins in a small pan and cover with a little water. Bring this to the boil, turn it off and let the raisins soak for half an hour.

Heat a heavy-bottomed frying pan, add a couple of tablespoons of olive oil and cook the bread on a high heat for about 30 seconds, then turn the heat down and cook the bread slowly – for about 20 minutes. Remove to a plate.

In the same pan heat a little olive oil and fry the spring onions or red onions for a couple of minutes. Add the pinenuts and brown for another minute or so. Drain the raisins and add them too. Turn off the heat and keep in a warm place.

When the chicken is cooked, remove from the roasting tray and place on an oven-proof dish, breast side up, and return to the oven to brown while you make the sauce. Put the roasting pan on a medium heat on top of the cooker and, when the juices start to bubble, add enough water to cover the vegetables, turn the heat to high and let the sauce bubble away until the liquid is reduced by half. Add the vinegars, stiring well, scraping the pan to dislodge all the tasty bits stuck to it. Let it simmer for a couple of minutes, strain into a bowl, taste and add more vinegar if needed.

When the chicken has browned in the oven, remove and joint it into eight portions.

Take a large serving dish, fill with the salad leaves, sprinkle the crisp bread (migas) and onion mixture on top and place the jointed chicken on top.

Serve with the vinegar sauce and bread to mop up the juices.

Pan-Fried Fish with Tomato, Caper and Herb Sauce, served with Rice and Fennel

4 x 250g of fish of your choice –
    any fish will be good here
½ recipe of tomato sauce from
    your freezer
200ml fish stock (page 49)
12 capers or chopped caper
    berries
Juice of a lemon
A big bunch of mixed herbs,
    such as tarragon, chives,
    dill and fennel
2 fennel bulbs

1 recipe of rice (page 29)

If your tomato sauce is not defrosted, you can do this by turning it out into a saucepan and putting a lid on over a low heat. If defrosted already, add the fish stock and let simmer for at least five minutes for the flavour to improve.

In the meantime, rinse the capers and chop if you are using the berries. Chop the herbs, not too fine, and squeeze the lemon. Add them to the tomato sauce. Mix well and taste, and season with salt and pepper if needed.

Bring a saucepan of water to the boil and cook the fennel bulbs until soft right through, about five to seven minutes.

In the meantime, heat a non-stick frying pan. Oil and season your fish with salt and pepper. When the pan is hot put in your fish, skin side down, and cook until the skin is nicely brown and the fish is starting to cook at the sides; this should take about four minutes. Turn and cook for another minute on the flesh side. Now let the fish rest for a minute.

Serve the fennel on top of the tomato sauce followed by the fish. Serve with a bowl of rice to pass around.

Notes

I love this dish, as I can change the sauce around depending how I am feeling and what I have. If I want it spicy, I can add some chilli or I can add some warm spices like some ground coriander, fennel and dill.

If I have some pesto or a big spoon of lime chutney that needs using, I can use it up here.

The Best Tasty Pork Chops

4 sprigs of rosemary

8 fat cloves garlic, peeled

Sea salt

Olive oil

4 good pork chops on the bone,
   with the skin left on

Juice of 2 lemons

1 recipe of potato cake
   (page 39)

Salad leaves

Olive oil

Maldon salt

A good heavy frying pan

Remove the chops from the fridge to come to room temperature. Take the needles from the stem of the rosemary and finely chop them with the garlic. Place in a bowl and mix with a good pinch of salt and enough olive oil to make a runny paste and rub this all over both sides of the pork chops. Leave to sit for at least 10 minutes. It will come to no harm if you want to do it in the morning, cover it, and leave in the fridge. Heat your oven to 160°/Gas 3.

Make the potato cake. Heat a frying pan until it is smoking with heat; you want your pan seriously hot here.

Put two of the chops in the pan, turn the heat down to a medium flame and let them sizzle nicely for about four minutes. Turn over and cook on the other side for another four minutes and transfer to the oven to keep warm while you cook the other two chops.

Press the meat that is closest to the bone and if it is firm and springy it is done. Leave to sit in the warm oven while you get everything else together and make the sauce.

Into the empty frying pan pour the lemon juice and swill it around to gather all the flavours and bits in the pan. Leave it on the heat until it all starts to bubble and reduces a little, then pour it over the chops.

When eating, remember to pick the bone; these are the tastiest bits.

Serve with the potato cake and green salad dressed with olive oil and Maldon salt.

Notes

This works well with chicken breasts and lamb chops.
Make the potato cake first and, as it is cooking in the oven,
cook the pork chops.

Lentil Salad with Mint and Feta Cheese, served with Baked Potato and Roasted Tomatoes

4 large baking potatoes or
   8 medium new potatoes
4 large ripe tomatoes
Salt and pepper
Olive oil

For the lentils

350g puy lentils
1 medium carrot, diced small
½ small onion, diced small
1 bay leaf
1 clove garlic, finely chopped
½ teaspoon salt
2tsp mint, chopped
3tbsp chopped mixed herbs –
   parsley, marjoram and chives
   or just parsley
Pepper
Cider vinegar, to taste
200–250g feta cheese

Lemon vinaigrette (see page 200)

Preheat the oven to its hottest temperature, place the potatoes on the highest oven shelf and bake for 45 minutes or until done.

In a saucepan put the lentils, carrots, onions, bay leaves, garlic and salt and cover well with water.

Bring to the boil and simmer until they are cooked.

This should only take about 25 minutes.

Halve the tomatoes, season with salt and pepper and drizzle with olive oil, put on a flat oven tray and place on the lowest shelf of the oven to roast for about 15 minutes.

In the meantime, make the lemon dressing (see page 200) by mixing all the ingredients together. I like to put everything in a jam jar with the lid on tightly and give it all a good shake.

Drain the lentils (keep the water for a soup). Add the lemon dressing while the lentils are still warm and mix in the mint and the rest of the herbs.

Taste and season with pepper and vinegar to lift the flavour.

Crumble the feta cheese and gently stir it into the lentils.

Serve the baked potatoes (with butter), roasted tomatoes and lentil salad along with a few green leaves or with some grilled streaky bacon.

Lemon Vinaigrette

Juice and fine zest of 1 large
    lemon or 2 small juicy lemons
½ tsp paprika
Pinch of cayenne pepper
1 clove garlic, minced
Salt
6–8 tbsp virgin olive oil

Mix all ingredients together in a bowl or in a jam jar with a lid and give a good shake.

Notes

If you have extra tomatoes that need using up, roast them as well and keep in the fridge for a sandwich or salad for lunch.
If the tomatoes do not have lots of flavour, they will taste so much better when roasted.
Puy lentils are the best for this dish, as they do hold their shape. Lentils are full of iron and vitamins, so eat plenty. This is one of the nicest ways to eat them as they are not heavy going and with the dressing and the salty cheese children love them!!!
Try this with the baked sweet potato with chilli butter on page 291.

Rice Noodles with Chicken

I packet of rice noodles

3 onions, halved and thinly sliced

Salt and pepper

1tbsp curry powder (mild or hot depending on taste)

1 x 400ml tin of coconut milk

All the pickings from the tarragon chicken from Sunday

Bunch of coriander, chopped (optional)

Bring a large saucepan of water to the boil for the noodles and heat a big frying pan or wok.

When the pan is hot add some oil and then the onions, season with salt and pepper and cook over a medium heat until nearly soft.

Add the curry powder, cook for another two minutes and pour in the coconut milk and bring to the boil. Let it simmer for a couple of minutes.

Add the shredded chicken and chopped coriander and mix well. Turn off the heat.

Cook the noodles in the boiling water, about 4 minutes for most, (some need to be soaked before cooking, so check the packet).

Drain the noodles, holding back a little of the water with them (to keep them moist).

Mix the noodles and sauce together well and serve.

Planning ahead

Cook the dish for tomorrow night.

Moroccan Lamb with Almonds and Raisins, served with Rice

This is a family favourite, just the dish when you want something bursting with flavour without much effort.

1kg shoulder lamb, cubed

Olive oil

2 medium onions, finely chopped

4 garlic cloves, finely chopped

Salt and pepper

2tsp turmeric

½tsp ground ginger

½tsp cayenne pepper

1 x 400g tin of tomatoes

300ml water

Some chopped parsley and
    coriander

200g raisins, soaked in water
    while you cook the meat

100g slivered almonds

1 recipe of rice (page 29)

A heavy-based saucepan that
    goes from hob to oven to
    table

In the saucepan place the meat, onions, garlic, salt, pepper and the spices along with four tablespoons of oil. Mix very well and add the tomatoes and water. Bring to the boil, reduce the heat, cover and let simmer for about 45 minutes. Add the drained raisins and herbs. Cook for another 30 minutes (without the lid) or until the meat is tender and the sauce looks like a thick gravy. (If you are cooking this a day in advance, cool now and keep in the fridge to reheat the next day.)

Preheat the oven to 180°/Gas 4.

Transfer the saucepan (without the lid) with the meat and bake in the oven for about 15 minutes until the meat is glazed. Meanwhile, heat a dry frying pan to toast the almonds over a medium flame and sprinkle over the top just before serving.

Serve with rice, which you have reheated by stirfrying in a hot pan, a salad of cucumber and onion (page 206) and a bowl of yoghurt.

Cucumber and Onion Salad

1 medium cucumber, diced
1 small onion, diced
Juice of ½ lemon
Salt and pepper
A splash of olive oil

Mix all ingredients together and season to taste with salt and pepper.

I vary the salad depending on what I have in the fridge, sometimes using up the ends of peppers, mango, spring onions and tomatoes.

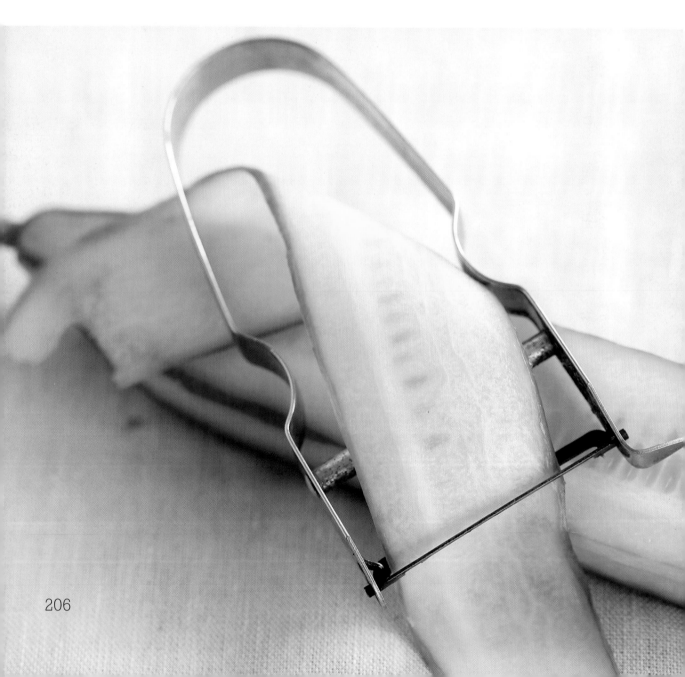

Week 7

Recipes

Shopping List

Supermarket

750ml unsweetened
   apple juice

Vegetables & Fruit

3kg Rooster potatoes
2.5kg new potatoes
8 onions
3 heads of garlic
1 celery
2 leeks
4 fennel bulbs
5 aubergines
1 head green cabbage
1 bunch spring onions
2 courgettes
2 red onions
7 red peppers
1 cucumber
4 large tomatoes
1 lemon
2 limes

2 oranges
Green salad
1 bag fresh spinach leaves
1 eating apple
2cm ginger
2 bunches parsley
1 bunch basil
1 bunch coriander
1 bunch mint

Dairy

75g feta cheese
500ml cream
6 eggs
100g Parmesan
250ml natural yoghurt

Fish Shop

4 x 250g hake fillets
4 x 250g haddock fillets

Butcher

2.5kg belly of pork with the
   rind scored
750g shoulder of lamb, minced
1kg shoulder of lamb, cubed

Other Shopping

Weekend Work for Week 7

Another short work list, which means there is time to make a nice dessert or a soup to have for lunch during the week. Tidy up the freezer and use anything which has been there for a while. This is a good way of checking what you have.

While the scones are baking, try a couple of dishes from the chapter 'A Few More Good Things'. Try the Piedmontese peppers on page 308; they would make a lovely starter if you are having friends for dinner. The St Emilion au chocolat on page 280 makes a real treat after a fish main course.

1 recipe of brown soda scones (page 25)
- *Allow them to cool and then freeze them.*

1 recipe of tomato sauce (page 44)
- for moussaka (page 221).
- *The rest can be frozen for a later date or kept in the fridge for a quick pasta or rice dish during the week.*

FROM THE FREEZER
200ml of fish stock (page 49)
- for braised fennel and leeks (page 217).

Roast Hake with Summer Vegetables and Herb Sauce

4 x 250g fillets of hake

Olive oil

Salt and pepper

4 large ripe tomatoes

2 courgettes

2 medium red onions

2 red peppers

Herb sauce

A big bunch parsley or a
  mixture of herbs

Olive oil

Salt and pepper

2 fat cloves of garlic

Serve with boiled new potatoes
  and green salad

Preheat the oven to its hottest, 250°/Gas 9, and preheat a shallow roasting tray big enough to take the vegetables. Prepare all the vegetables: quarter the tomatoes, courgettes, red onions and peppers and put in a mixing bowl; coat well in olive oil and season well with salt and pepper.

Remove the very hot tray from the oven and pour on your vegetables, spreading them out. Return to the oven and roast for about 25 minutes or until the vegetables are soft and a little charred.

In the meantime, boil the kettle and use the water to boil the potatoes. Let them cook while you make the herb sauce and cook the fish.

Make the sauce by chopping the parsley and garlic finely and mixing with enough olive oil to make a paste. Season with salt and pepper.

Lightly oil and season the fish.

Place the seasoned fish on top of the vegetables and return to the oven.

Let the fish cook at the high heat for about eight to 10 minutes or until soft to the touch in the centre. Do not overcook; check after six minutes.

Serve from the tray with a bowl of potatoes and the salad leaves dressed with oil and salt.

Roast Belly of Pork with Pickled Prunes and Sweet and Sour Cucumber, served with Roast Potatoes

2.5kg pork belly, rind scored
2 onions, with skins on
2 celery sticks
2 bay leaves
1 head of garlic
500ml apple juice
2tbsp fennel seeds
2tbsp coriander seeds
2tbsp chopped rosemary
Salt and pepper
Oil

For the pickled prunes
250ml cider vinegar
300g sugar
1 stick cinnamon, broken
6 juniper berries, crushed
    between your fingers
1tbsp sugar
2 whole cloves
500g prunes
    (good quality unpitted)

For the cucumber
1 medium cucumber
1tbsp flaked sea salt
1tbsp cider vinegar
1½tbsp sugar

1 recipe roast potatoes (page 43)
1 recipe gravy (page 34)

Preheat the oven to 250°/Gas 9.

Pound or crush the spices and mix with the chopped rosemary, salt, pepper and enough oil to make a runny paste. Rub it all over the flesh of the pork, avoiding the skin on top. Season the skin well with salt and pepper.

Roughly chop the celery, onions (skins on) and garlic, spread on a roasting tray with the bay leaves and lay the pork on top. Roast in the preheated oven for about an hour. You want the skin to be nicely crackled and brown.

Turn the oven down to 180°/Gas 6 and cook for another hour. At this stage get the potatoes under way.

While the meat is cooking make the pickled prunes by putting all the ingredients into a saucepan and bringing slowly to the boil as you stir it to help dissolve the sugar. When it reaches the boil, turn the heat down to low and let it simmer gently for 15 minutes. Leave to cool and serve at room temperature.

Next prepare the cucumber. Slice the cucumber as thinly as you can and mix with the salt, sugar and vinegar.

Remove the meat from the roasting tray and keep warm while you make the gravy. Pour in the apple juice and top up the tray with tap water, making sure all the vegetables are well covered, and bring to the boil. Let it boil for about five minutes on the top of the cooker. Turn the heat down and let simmer for at least 15 minutes, until the gravy reduces a little and the flavour improves. Pour into a serving bowl through a sieve, keeping back the vegetables.

Give the vegetables a good press down to help push through all the liquid.

Slice the meat into thick slices and serve with the prunes, cucumber, gravy and roast potatoes.

Notes

Carving – you might find it easier to remove the crackled skin first, cut it up and then cut the meat.

If you have time, let the pork sit (marinate) with the spice mixture for about an hour, as the flavour will be better.

This recipe will work using a leg or shoulder (on the bone) of pork, which I like to do for a big party.

The prunes and cucumber would turn a plain roast shoulder or leg of pork or baked pork chops into an interesting meal.

The prunes will keep in the fridge for at least three weeks.

The cucumber goes well with cold meats and pan-fried fish.

Adapted from Diana Henry's book Roast Figs Sugar Snow, *a book full of comfort food.*

Planning ahead

Keep extra pork and gravy for the stirfry on page 225.

Pan-fried Fish with Braised Fennel and Leeks, served with Potato Cake

4 x 250g fish fillets (haddock or pollock), skin on and scales removed

1 recipe of braised fennel and leeks (page 218)

Serve with potato cake (page 39) or boiled potatoes

Prepare the recipe for braised fennel and leeks.
Prepare the potato cake or, for an easier life, just boil some potatoes. When the potatoes are cooked, heat your frying pan until very hot. Oil and season the fish on a plate.
In the very hot dry pan place the fish skin side down and cook for about four or five minutes on this side without moving the fillet. Keep an eye on the heat; you might need to turn the heat down a little. Now turn the fillet over and finish cooking on the flesh side for about two minutes. This will depend on the thickness of the fillet; try not to overcook it.
Serve with the braised fennel and potato cake.

Braised Fennel and Leeks

4 fennel bulbs
2 medium leeks
Salt and pepper
Olive oil to coat the bottom
    of the pan
200ml fish stock (page 49),
    water or white wine
½tsp fennel seeds
½tsp coriander seeds

A medium saucepan

Cut each fennel bulb into quarters, splitting it from top to
bottom. Slice the leeks lengthways, wash well and chop.
Heat the oil in a large casserole, add the fennel and some
seasoning and allow the bulbs to 'fry' in the oil until lightly
coloured. Fennel spits when cooked in oil, so be careful.
Turn the fennel gently and cook the other side.
Mix in the leeks and fennel seeds. Stir and cook for a couple
of minutes and add the fish stock or water.
Cover and cook over a low heat until the fennel is soft when
pricked with a knife. About 10 to 15 minutes.
Season with salt and pepper.
Serve with pan-fried fish.

Notes

*Sometimes I vary the fennel recipe by adding some mild spices
such as coriander, fennel or dill and some lemon zest.
Fennel, boiled and seasoned with salt and pepper and a good
sprinkle of Parmesan cheese and baked in an oiled dish in the
oven or given a few minutes under a hot grill is a lovely side
dish for pan-fried fish or meat.*

Moussaka with Green Salad

Moussaka is one of my favourite dishes, really because aubergines are one of my favourite vegetables and also, as it is one of those dishes that is complete in itself, you just need a green salad on the side.

Olive oil

750g minced lamb

Salt and pepper

1tsp cumin seeds

½ recipe of tomato sauce from the freezer

½ cinnamon stick

1 heaped tsp dried oregano

3 large aubergines, cut into slices at least 5mm thick

Salt and pepper

For the topping

75g feta cheese, crumbled

2 whole eggs

2 egg yolks

500ml double cream

Big bunch of parsley and mint, chopped

40g Parmesan

Zest of 1 lemon

Pepper

Preheat the oven to its hottest and heat up a flat oven tray. Heat about two tablespoons of oil in a pan. Season the meat well with salt, pepper and cumin and cook the lamb for a few minutes until it is lightly browned.

Add the tomato sauce to the lamb along with the cinnamon stick and the oregano and simmer gently for 30 minutes.

In the meantime toss the aubergines in a large mixing bowl with salt and pepper and mix in a good splash of oil. Remove the hot tray from the oven, spread out the aubergines and roast in the oven for 10–15 minutes or until the aubergines are soft and slightly brown. Turn the oven down to 200°/Gas 6.

For the topping, mix the eggs, egg yolks, cream, herbs, lemon zest and Parmesan together and season with black pepper. Take an ovenproof dish (2-litre), lay half of the aubergines on the bottom followed by the lamb sauce and cover with the rest of the aubergines. Pour the topping over it and sprinkle the feta on top.

Bake in the oven for 25–30 minutes or until bubbling.

Serve with a green salad dressed with olive oil and Maldon salt and new potatoes/bread.

Notes

You can replace the aubergines with potatoes or courgettes. For potatoes, treat in the same way as aubergines or simply slice the potatoes, rinse well in water and boil or steam until just soft in the centre.

For courgettes, the same as for aubergines but much less cooking or lightly boil or steam. Courgettes (pan-fried) work well here, as they do not soak up oil like aubergines.

Flour-based Cheese Sauce

60g butter
60g plain flour
600ml full-cream milk
Salt and pepper
3 medium eggs
75g feta cheese
40g grated Parmesan

Bring the milk to the boil.

In another saucepan, melt the butter, stir in the flour and cook for two minutes on a low heat without browning – this needs a little patience!

Gradually stir in the boiled milk, whisking all time, taking it off and on the heat as you whisk.

Return to the heat and leave to cook for a few minutes on a low heat.

Season to taste with salt and pepper.

Lightly beat the eggs in a bowl and add to the sauce, mixing in well. Fold in the cheese.

Notes

When I am not in a rush, I like to boil the milk with a chopped small onion, carrot, a bay leaf and a stick of celery and let it sit for 30 minutes, pouring it through a sieve before using.

Stirfry of Green Cabbage, Apple, Ginger, Pumpkin Seeds and Pork, served with Rice Noodles

2 medium onions, sliced finely

½ head of medium green
   cabbage, sliced finely

Salt and pepper

1 x 2–3cm thumb of fresh ginger,
   peeled and grated on a plate

Zest of 1 orange

For the sauce

6 cloves of garlic

1 fresh chilli, finely chopped

2 limes, juiced

100ml tamari or soy sauce

All of your leftover gravy or
   250ml of apple juice

1 bunch spring onions

To finish off

Cooked belly of pork

1 eating apple, cored and sliced

30g pumpkin seeds, toasted in
   a dry pan

Fresh coriander (optional)

Serve with rice noodles

Soak the rice noodles in cold water.

Bring a saucepan of water to the boil.

Remove the leftover cooked pork from the fridge, to bring to room temperature, and cut into eight slices.

Heat a wok or a large frying pan until it starts to smoke.

If using the pumpkin seeds, toast quickly in the dry wok or pan and keep to one side.

Add a little oil followed by the sliced onions, orange zest and grated ginger and cook for a couple of minutes until the onions soften a little. Next add the sliced cabbage, some salt and pepper. Stir well and let cook for about five minutes – sometimes I add a couple of tablespoons of water to help the cooking. In the meantime, make the sauce by mixing together the chopped garlic, chilli, lime juice, tamari and gravy.

Add the sauce to the stirfry, mix well, cook for a minute, add the apple and the pumpkin seeds and lay the pork slices on top. Let them warm through for a few minutes without mixing them in (sometimes I speed this up by covering the pan with foil for a couple of minutes).

Add the noodles to the boiling water and cook for the stated time on the packet, usually two or three minutes. Drain off the water, retaining a little of the cooking liquid, toss in a little oil and mix well.

Sprinkle the stirfry with the coriander and serve with the noodles.

Notes

Do not heat the pork too much, as it will toughen and dry out.

Fettuccine with Spinach, Roasted Peppers and Saffron Butter

The saffron butter:

100g butter

2 cloves of garlic, finely diced

8 basil leaves, roughly chopped

1tbsp parsley leaves, roughly
   chopped

8 saffron threads soaked in
   1tsp hot water

Pinch cayenne pepper

Grated zest of 1 lime or zest
   of ½ orange

½ tsp salt

The sauce

3 medium red peppers, halved,
   cored and sliced thinly

Olive oil

1 big bunch fresh spinach,
   washed

50g pinenuts

1 onion, quartered and thinly
   sliced

300ml water or vegetable stock
   (if you have it)

3 cloves garlic, finely chopped

½ tsp salt

Pepper

Parmesan to sprinkle

500g fettuccine

Cream the butter with the rest of the ingredients for the saffron butter and set aside until needed.

Heat a medium saucepan (with a lid) and add a good splash of olive oil. Add the sliced onions and red peppers and season with salt and pepper.

Turn the heat to low, put on the lid and cook until soft, which should take about eight to 10 minutes.

Stem the spinach. Finely chop the stems and add to the onion and pepper mixture. Cook for a couple of minutes. Roughly chop the leaves.

Toast the pinenuts under the grill or in a dry pan over a medium heat until golden.

Put the pasta on to cook.

Add the water or stock and garlic to the pepper mixture, bring to the boil and let simmer for a minute. Add the spinach and mix well until all the spinach is wilted.

Lower the heat and add the saffron butter.

Drain the pasta, keeping back about a tablespoon of the cooking water.

Mix the pasta, the tablespoon of cooking water and the vegetable sauce and sprinkle with the toasted pinenuts.

Serve with Parmesan and black pepper.

Notes

You can vary the butter flavouring.

Use shallots instead of garlic.

Use a mixture of herbs such as chives, marjoram and tarragon instead of basil.

If you find saffron too expensive, add more lemon or orange zest or a mixture of both and add a pinch of nutmeg.

Saffron and orange go really well together.

Don't ever throw out the stalks of the spinach; they just need a little longer cooking than the leaves. I use them all the time in stirfries, cooked and mixed in with rice, and boiled, drained and sprinkled on a pizza.

Planning ahead

Cook the dish for tomorrow evening.

Lamb and Mint Pilaf with Cherry Compote, served with Roasted Red Pepper and Aubergines

Olive oil

1kg cubed shoulder of lamb

2 onions, chopped

2 small tsp ground cinnamon

A knob of butter, or olive oil if
you prefer

175g bulgar wheat (or couscous
or rice)

350ml water

Leaves from a small bunch of
mint, torn

For the compote

200g caster sugar

250ml water

½ cinnamon stick

200g dried sour cherries

Juice of 1 lime

1tbsp rosewater (optional)

To serve

250ml natural yoghurt

3 fat cloves of garlic

Salt and pepper

Heat a frying pan until it is very hot. In the meantime turn the lamb into a bowl, mix in two tablespoons of oil and season well with salt and pepper, giving it a good mix around. You might need a drop more oil. You want all the lamb to have a light coating.

In the very hot pan brown the meat on all sides. You will more than likely have to do this in at least two batches. Do not over-crowd the pan, as the meat will not brown. As you brown the meat, remove it from the pan and set it aside. When all the meat is browned, add a little oil to the pan and cook the onion until soft and starting to colour a little.

Add the cinnamon and cook with the onion for a minute. Return the meat to the pan, cover with water and bring it all up to the boil. Turn the heat down low and cook for about an hour or until the meat is tender.

While the meat is cooking, make the compote. Put the sugar, cinnamon and water in a saucepan and bring it slowly to the boil. Stir from time to time to help the sugar melt. Boil for about five minutes, then add the cherries and continue to cook slowly for 15 minutes. Let the cherries cool and add the lime juice and rosewater.

If you're making this in advance, you can stop now, allow the lamb and the compote to cool and put them in the fridge. Then you can reheat the lamb the next day and continue.

In a heavy-based saucepan (with a lid) melt some butter with some olive oil. When it is nicely foaming add the bulgar and mix well for a few minutes, letting it toast a little.

To the bulgar add the lamb along with its liquid and bring to the boil. Then turn down very low, cover and cook for about 15 minutes. Remove from the heat.

In the meantime, chop the garlic, mix it into the yoghurt and season with salt and pepper.

Fork the bulgar and the lamb together, add the chopped mint and serve with the compote and the yoghurt.

Notes

If you want to avoid wheat, use rice instead. Take 250g short grain brown rice and treat it the same way as the bulgar but cook it with the lamb for 30 minutes.

You will have extra cherry compote, which will keep in the fridge for at least a month, and you can use it with lamb chops or roast lamb.

Roasted Red Peppers and Aubergines

2 red peppers, quartered and
    seeds removed
1 large aubergine, sliced
Olive oil
Salt and pepper

Flat roasting tray

Heat the oven to its hottest and warm the oven tray.

Put the chopped vegetables into a mixing bowl. Pour in enough oil to coat all the vegetables and season well with salt and pepper.

Take the hot tray from the oven, spread the oiled vegetables evenly on it and return to the top of the oven and cook for 20 to 30 minutes or until the vegetables are cooked and just starting to char a little.

Week 8

Recipes

Shopping List

Supermarket

Vegetables & Fruit
2.5kg Rooster potatoes
1.5kg new potatoes
4 onions or 2 large
4 garlic bulbs
3 red onions
3 red peppers
7 carrots
3 aubergines
6 courgettes
16 tomatoes, large
2 leeks, medium
1 bunch spring greens
  or spinach
1 green pepper, large
1 bunch spring onions
2 small beetroot
6 lemons
2 lime
1 pack of red chillies

2 oranges
4 heads of salad
3 bunches parsley
3 bunches coriander
  or parsley
1 cucumber

Dairy
1 litre natural yoghurt

Fish Shop

8 mackerel
4 x 250g pollock

Butcher

1 chicken
4 whole chicken legs or
  4 lamb shoulder chops
750g minced beef (lean)

Other Shopping

Weekend Work for Week 8

This weekend you will be so bored you could use your time to stock up your fridge with some snacks for lunch during the week. Try the hummus on page 304. The Gazpacho on page 269 is great to have in the fridge, especially when the sun is shining. You could also give the chocolate and banana cake on page 319 a go (double the recipe and freeze one for later).

1 recipe of brown soda scones (page 25)

Remember to defrost any chicken bones you have in the freezer to make a chicken stock on Sunday evening.

Pan-fried or BBQ Mackerel with Orange Salsa, New Potatoes and Green Salad

8 medium mackerel
A pot of new potatoes
A bowl of salad leaves
Olive oil
Salt and pepper

For the salsa

2 oranges, segmented (save
    juice for dressing) and
    chopped finely
1 small red onion, chopped finely
½ cucumber, chopped finely
1 red pepper, chopped finely
1 red chilli, with seeds,
    chopped finely
Small bunch of parsley
Juice of 1 lemon
Salt and pepper
Olive oil

Firstly, make the salsa by mixing together all the ingredients. Season well with salt and pepper and add enough olive oil to bring together. Boil the potatoes.
Heat a large frying pan until it smokes.
Oil the fish very well all over and place in the very hot pan.
Once the fish is in the pan, do not move or turn it for about five minutes until it is well cooked on the first side (or you will break the skin). Turn over and cook for just a minute more if small and two minutes if medium. Remove from the pan to a serving plate and sprinkle the salsa on top. Dress the salad leaves with olive oil, salt and pepper. Toss and serve.

Other ways of serving mackerel

– Grilled tomatoes and a horseradish cream made by mixing two tablespoons of horseradish sauce with 200ml of sour cream seasoned with salt and pepper.
– Stewed gooseberries – top and tail and stew over a low heat with 1 tablespoon water and two tablespoons sugar. Gooseberries freeze well, so keep them until mackerel is available.
– Stewed rhubarb – stew with a little sugar and lemon juice until soft but still holding its shape, add one red deseeded chilli, stir and leave to cool.

Notes

Buy mackerel fillets if you prefer them to whole and cook for just two minutes on the skin side and one minute on the flesh side.
Bake mackerel fillets in the oven with a topping of chopped garlic, pinenuts, lemon juice and finely grated zest of lemon, a handful of chopped parsley, a little rosemary, chopped finely, and a quarter of a medium onion, diced, and a scattering of capers.
To segment an orange can be tricky. If you have not done this before, just peel the orange by hand, segment it and chop the segments small with a sharp knive.

Roast Chicken with Pumpkin-Seed Stuffing, served with Ratatouille and Potatoes

Chicken – the best you can buy

Olive oil

Salt and pepper

3 bay leaves

1 large onion, chopped with the
   skin on

2 celery sticks, roughly chopped

2 carrots, roughly chopped

50g pumpkin seeds

Big handful of fresh coriander

2 garlic cloves

2 spring onions

1 chilli, with seeds
   (for a little heat)

Zest and juice of 1 lime

Set the oven at 250°/Gas 9.

Take the pumpkin seeds, coriander, garlic, spring onions, chilli and lime zest and chop as finely as you can with a sharp knife or put in a food processor and whiz until you have a paste. Add in the lime juice and bring it all together. Gently loosen the skin of the chicken away from the breast and leg meat with your hand and push the pumpkin-seed stuffing in under the loose skin, making sure you spread it down into the legs. Smooth the skin down, making sure the stuffing is well spread out underneath.

Take a roasting tin with sides no deeper than 5cm and fill with chopped vegetables. Lay the chicken, breast-side down, on top of the vegetables. Roast for an hour at the high heat.

If you have a fan oven, do keep an eye as you might have to turn the heat down or move the tin to the centre of the oven. Boil the kettle to cook the pototoes and heat the tomato sauce to make the ratatouille.

Transfer the chicken to an ovenproof plate or tray, turning the bird the right way up to brown the skin. Return the bird to the hot oven to brown while you make the gravy (see page 34). The chicken is ready when the juices run clear. Remove it from the oven and let it rest for 10 minutes.

Quick Ratatouille

2 aubergines

4 courgettes

1 recipe of tomato sauce
   (page 44) (defrosted from
   the freezer)

Heat the tomato sauce over a medium heat. Slice the vegetables. Add the aubergines to the sauce, reduce the heat and let simmer for five minutes, then add the courgettes and cook for another five minutes or until all the vegetables are soft.

Planning ahead

Defrost chicken bones and make a big pot of stock, letting it simmer as you are doing the dishes.

Spicy Roast Fish, Potatoes and Tomatoes, served with Green Salad

4 x 250g pollock, skin on
    and scaled
750g potatoes
8 fresh tomatoes
Salt and pepper
Olive oil

Marinade

4 garlic cloves
1tsp cumin seeds
1tsp smoked paprika
½tsp ground chilli powder
4tbsp olive oil
Juice of 1 lemon

Salad leaves
Maldon salt
Olive oil

Heat the oven to 240°/Gas 9 and heat a low-sided oven tray. Mix everything for the marinade together in a bowl, add the fish and cover well with the marinade.

While the fish is marinating, peel the potatoes and cut into big chunks, toss into a large mixing bowl, along with the chopped tomatoes, season well with salt and pepper and add a good splash of oil, making sure all the vegetables are well coated. Spread out evenly on the preheated tray and roast for 20–30 minutes or until the potatoes are soft when tested with a knife. After about 15 minutes give everything a good mix on the tray to help the tomatoes to release their juices.

Take the vegetables out of the oven and place the fish fillets on top, skin side up. Pour the leftover marinade around the fish and return it to the oven.

Bake for about eight to 10 minutes or until the fish is cooked through (check by pressing the thickest part of the fish with your finger; if it is soft to the touch, it is cooked).

Serve with a green salad dressed with a little olive oil and a sprinkle of Maldon salt.

Barley, Potato and Chicken Stew

150g pearl barley

3 sprigs fresh thyme

1 litre chicken stock

4 large cooked potatoes, chopped into bite-sized pieces

2 medium leeks, finely sliced

½ Savoy cabbage, shredded

1 bunch spring greens or spinach, shredded

Any meat saved from the chicken carcass (optional)

Salt

Ground black pepper

Bunch of parsley, chopped

Put the barley and thyme in a large pan, cover with cold water, bring to the boil and simmer for about 30 minutes. Drain. Return to the pan, add the chicken stock and bring back to a simmer.

After about 20 minutes, test the barley – if it's nearly done, it should still have a little bite. Add the leeks and let them simmer for another five minutes until just tender. Add the cabbage and greens and cook for two or three minutes, until tender. Add the chicken meat and potato right at the end. Season to taste, sprinkle with the chopped parsley and serve at once.

Notes

To make this dish vegetarian, use a vegetable stock. Instead of the chicken add tofu and finish off with finely sliced spring onions, grated carrot, thin sticks of cucumber and an interesting mix of herbs such as coriander, basil and tarragon.

Leftover cooked lamb can be used instead of chicken and some fresh mint sprinkled on at the end with the parsley.

Roast Vegetables with Yoghurt Sauce and Zhug, served with Couscous

2 red peppers, cut into 8 pieces

1 large aubergine

8 tomatoes, halved

1 red onion, quartered

2 courgettes

90ml (6tbsp) olive oil

Salt and pepper

For the yoghurt sauce

400ml natural yoghurt

2 garlic cloves

Salt and pepper

For the Zhug

3 hot red chillies, deseeded
  if you don't do hot!

Seeds from 8 cardamom pods

7.5ml (1½tsp) caraway seeds,
  crushed

3 garlic cloves, chopped finely

A large bunch of coriander,
  stalks and leaves chopped
  finely

100ml extra-virgin olive oil

A good squeeze of fresh lime
  juice to taste

1 recipe of couscous (page 32)

Roast the vegetables by heating a flat oven tray in a very hot oven. Prepare all the vegetables, put them into a large mixing bowl and season with salt and pepper. Add a good splash of oil, mix well and spread evenly on the hot tray. Return to the oven and roast for 25 to 30 minutes or until soft and nicely charred.

Make the yoghurt sauce, by chopping the garlic finely and mixing into the yoghurt, and season with the salt and pepper. Next make the Zhug, by chopping the chillies finely and mixing with the spices, garlic and coriander. Add the olive oil and lemon juice and mix well. You can use a food processor if you have one. Whiz up the chillies with the spices and coriander and feed in the juice and oil to make a paste.

When your vegetables are ready, spoon the yoghurt around them on the tray and serve with the Zhug (in a bowl for people to help themselves) along with a big pot of couscous, or rice if you prefer.

Notes

Extra Zhug in the fridge can be used to spice up many dishes in the weeks to come. Add to baked potatoes, grilled lamb or pork or just mix into a bowl of rice.

You can use any mixture of vegetables you like. I often make this dish in winter with carrots, parsnip, sweet potatoes and white onions.

Baked Smoked-Paprika Chicken, served with Potatoes and Carrot, Beetroot and Seed Salad

This style of cooking is so great and can be adapted to use many different ingredients. twenty minutes in the kitchen will produce a great dish to place on the table.

4 whole chicken legs or a
    whole chicken, jointed
2tsp smoked paprika
4 fat cloves garlic
About 750g–1kg potatoes
Olive oil
Salt and pepper

1 recipe of carrot, beetroot
    and seed salad (page 251)

Heat the oven to its hottest and heat a shallow roasting tray, about 2–3cm deep, towards the top of the oven.

Peel and slice the potatoes about 1cm thick, put into a big mixing bowl, add enough oil just to coat them all and season with salt and pepper. Mix well, making sure all the potatoes are nicely coated with the oil.

Remove the tray from the oven and spread out the sliced potatoes (they will overlap a little).

In the same mixing bowl, put in the chicken along with the smoked paprika, garlic, a little olive oil and a good pinch of salt and pepper. Mix well, rubbing the seasoning into the chicken.

Lay the chicken on top of the potatoes and return to the oven. Bake at the high heat for 20 minutes then turn the oven down to 200°/Gas 6 and cook for at least another 20 minutes or until the potatoes are soft when you test the ones in the middle of the tray and the juices from the chicken run clear.

Notes

I prefer to buy a whole chicken and portion it up and then have the bones for a stock. Ask your butcher to do this for you. Also try flavouring the chicken with turmeric, a small pinch of chilli powder, three cardamom pods, crushed, and a few strands of saffron (dissolved in a teaspoon of water) and sprinkle the finished dish with some soaked raisins and toasted pinenuts.

I find this recipe works even better with lamb shoulder chops.

*Mix in some cumin seeds with the smoked paprika. I like to cook
these really well until the lamb is starting to crisp at the edges.
Last week my brother wanted a fast dish that would also tempt
his two young boys, who have a sweet tooth, so I suggested that
he adapt Diana Henry's dish of hot lightning. Cover the tray with
sliced potatoes, apples and pears, sprinkle on lots of chopped
thyme, some salt and pepper. Lay the seasoned pork chops on
top and bake until the pork starts to crisp at the edges and the
potatoes in the centre of the tray are soft. It was a big hit with
everybody.*

*When I am lazy and do not want to make the salad, I roast
halved tomatoes, sprinkled with salt, pepper and olive oil, on a
tray towards the bottom of the oven while the meat is cooking.
I place them around the meat on the tray and serve.*

Carrot, Beetroot and Seed Salad

For the dressing

100ml lemon juice

1tsp sugar

3tbsp olive oil

Salt and pepper

For the salad

100g mixed seeds (pumpkin,
   sunflower, linseed or sesame)

4 medium-sized carrots

2 small or medium-sized
   beetroots

Put the lemon juice in a small mixing bowl with half a teaspoon of sea salt and several grinds of coarse black pepper. Stir in the sugar until it dissolves, then add the olive oil and set aside. Put the pumpkin, sunflower and linseed or sesame seeds into a dry frying pan and cook over a moderate heat until they smell nutty and are starting to turn a toasty gold in colour. Remove from the heat.

Scrub the carrots and grate coarsely. Toss them quickly into the dressing so that they don't have time to discolour. Peel and trim the beetroots, cut them into quarters and grate them. Toss them with the carrot and the toasted seeds. Check the seasoning.

Planning ahead

Make chilli for tomorrow night. If not using tinned beans, remember to soak the dried beans tonight.

Chilli Con Carne with Bean Salad, Rice and Yoghurt

This is based on Jane Grigson's recipe for chilli from her Vegetable Book.

750g lean minced beef
Olive oil
1 large onion, chopped
4 cloves of garlic, crushed
Colorado sauce (p. 253) or
    1tsp chilli powder
1tbsp tomato concentrate
1tbsp cumin seeds
Salt and pepper
1 large green pepper, finely
    chopped
A pinch of brown sugar
400g tin red kidney beans
400ml natural yoghurt

A heavy-based saucepan

Heat the pan until hot and add some olive oil. Add the onions, season with salt and pepper and cook on a medium heat until soft (about five minutes).

In the meantime, season the meat with salt and pepper, mixing it in well, and add to the cooked onions. Increase the heat to brown the meat, mixing well to help break up the meat. Add the garlic, Colorado sauce and just enough water to cover the ingredients. Cover tightly and leave to stew until cooked, keeping the heat low (for about an hour) – or pop it in a low oven. By the end of the cooking time it should have reduced to a brownish-red thick sauce. If it reduces too soon because the lid of the pan is not a tight fit, or you had the heat too high, top it up with water.

Add the tomato concentrate (the kidney beans if you are not serving them separately as a salad), with salt and brown sugar to taste.

Simmer for a further 15 minutes, add the chopped pepper and serve with rice, bean salad and yoghurt. The flavour is better if made a day ahead and even better served with a cold beer.

Colorado Sauce

2 small dried red chillies,
   or 3 large fresh ones
1 large red pepper
1 large onion, chopped
1 large clove garlic
Salt

If the chillies are dried, soak them in a little boiling water for 10 minutes. Discard the stalks.

Chop up the red pepper and purée with the other ingredients, using the soaking water if necessary to moisten the vegetables. If you use fresh chillies you might need a tablespoon or two of cold water. Season with salt. You can chop it all very fine by hand or by putting in the food processor or by using a soup whizzer.

You can keep this sauce in a covered container in the fridge for four or five days, or you can freeze it.

Bean Salad

400g tin kidney beans
400g tin chickpeas
1 bunch spring onions,
    chopped finely
3 cloves garlic
Lots of chopped parsley
6tbsp olive oil
Juice of 1 large lemon
Salt, pepper and sugar

Mix all the ingredients except the beans in a serving bowl, and season to taste with salt, pepper and sugar.
Rinse the beans under running water. Bring a saucepan of water to the boil and heat the rinsed beans for a minute, drain and toss into the dressing and mix well. Leave to cool.
Keeps well in the fridge for 3 days

Notes

A bowl of avocado salsa would be a nice addition to the chilli. Just dice the avocado and a small red onion, add the juice of one lime, salt, pepper and a little olive oil to bind it.
Kidney beans are not my favourite beans. I find that they don't take on flavour as much as the others, so if I don't have them in the cupboard I use butter beans instead. However, the kidney beans do add colour to the salad.
To cook your own beans is nicer, but I nearly always forget to soak them the night before!!!

Vegetarian chilli

Take two tins of your favourite beans and mix them together. Follow the above recipe, leaving out the meat and adding the beans to the softened onions in the saucepan. Then add the rest of the ingredients but reduce the cooking time to 30 minutes.

Soups

Soups

Here are eight soups to try, one for each week. They are all very simple, easy, quick and good enough to stand alone with good bread.

If you have a few onions and a potato, add a few spices and you have a meal. A bowl of soup is pure comfort food and so versatile. You can have it for lunch, dinner, starter, main course, in a posh soup bowl or from your favourite mug. It tastes great served from a flask after a long walk, or on a long journey where you would otherwise be disappointed stopping on the gastronomic desert of a motorway!

Soups are a great way of using up the bits and pieces that lurk in the bottom of your fridge or that tin of beans, lentils or coconut milk which has made its way to the back of the cupboard. When I tidy my cupboards, I very often soak all the odd bits of beans overnight and make them into a soup with some tinned tomatoes while livening it up with a few spices.

Most soups work well without a stock; all you need is tap water. There is no need for a stock cube or powder. Make sure to season well at the start of the cooking. Let the vegetables sweat with a lid on for as long as possible before adding the water. Remember to taste as it cooks and add more seasoning if necessary.

The soups are all dairy-free and flour-free (except the chowder). Soups made this way are lighter and tastier.

For most soups I use a general base of vegetables, as in the turnip and ginger soup on page 268, and then add my main ingredient, depending on what is in season.

Vegetable Soup with Parsley Pesto

There are no set amounts for this soup. You are working by eye and with what you have.

Variety of vegetables:
onions, celery, fennel,
parsnips, turnip and carrots.
You could omit any of these
(with the exception of the
onion), and include celeriac,
courgette or even shredded
Savoy cabbage

Salt

Pepper

Heat a heavy-based saucepan. When warm add a good splash of olive oil.

Chop all the vegetables – keeping the turnip and parsnip to one side – into small dice. Add to the warm oil and toss well, making sure they are well coated. At this point season with salt and freshly ground black pepper.

Cover the pan and sweat the vegetables until they are soft and have produced a liquid. The longer you leave them to sweat, the better the flavour of your soup. Each time you lift the lid, let the liquid which has condensed on it fall back into the pot.

If you are using turnip and parsnips, add them at this stage, as they contain starch.

Cover the vegetables with water.

Cook for about 30 minutes, add the cabbage and cook until the vegetables are soft. At this point you can buzz-gun or purée the soup in a food processor to make it smooth, but after all that nice chopping I like to leave it as it is. On the other hand, whizzing it up hides the unpopular vegetable. If you are going to purée, just roughly chop everything.

Parsley Pesto

4 large cloves of garlic
Salt
A big bunch of parsley –
     about 3 big handfuls
Olive oil

Chop the garlic and parsley very fine, mix together in a bowl
and add a good pinch of salt.
Add in olive oil until you get a pesto the consistency of thick
mayonnaise.
Serve this with the soup. It can be added at the table to taste.

Sweet Red Pepper Soup

This recipe is based on Elizabeth David's recipe for the Catalan soup, Majorquina, from her cookbook Mediterranean Food. *Serves 4–5.*

Olive oil

1 sprig of fresh thyme

2 bay leaves

2 cloves

1 small dried chilli

4 cloves garlic, chopped

1 medium onion, sliced

700g red peppers, seeded
   and sliced

Salt and pepper

1 x 400g tin plum tomatoes

200g Savoy or green cabbage,
   chopped

Slowly warm a heavy-based saucepan, add a good splash of the olive oil and warm the thyme, bay leaves and cloves until they are aromatic. Add the garlic and chilli and cook for about half a minute, without letting it brown; then stir in the onion and the peppers and season well with salt and pepper. Stir well to coat the vegetables with the oil, cover the pot and leave on a flame tamer over a very low heat.

Check the pot after 10 minutes and give it a stir. If the vegetables are sticking add a splash of water and continue cooking for another five to 10 minutes.

Add the tomatoes and 1.5 litres of water. Bring to the boil then lower the heat to a slow simmer. Add the cabbage and cook on a medium heat for another 10 minutes.

Let the soup cool a little, remove the bay leaves and whizz up until it is smooth.

To posh it up
Serve with a bowl of sour cream, lime segments and a salsa.

Notes
You could use tinned pepper instead of fresh.

Onion and Cider Soup

Serves 4

100g butter
1.5kg onions,
    halved and sliced thinly
Salt and pepper
250ml cider
1.2 litres chicken stock
Leaves from 3 sprigs fresh thyme
8 slices bread, toasted – optional
8 slices of strong cheddar
    cheese that melts well

Melt the butter in a heavy-bottomed saucepan, add the onions and season. Sauté them gently, turning them around in the butter until they start to soften. Cover with a lid, reduce the heat as low as possible and sweat the onions until they are very soft. This can take up to 50 minutes.

Take the lid off and turn the heat up to medium so that the juices can evaporate and the onions caramelise.

When the onions are nice and golden, add the cider, stock and thyme and bring to the boil. Simmer for 15 minutes (the soup can be made to this stage, cooled and stored until needed, then brought back to the boil and finished off as below).

Ladle the soup into bowls and put a slice of toast on top of each bowl. Lay the slices of cheese on top and heat under the grill until golden and bubbling.

Serve immediately.

Notes

If you need to skip the bread, just lay the cheese on top of the soup and melt.

Chowder

Serves 4–6 people.

500g smoked haddock (or just
    some nice fresh fish),
    chopped
25g butter
50g sliced green streaky
    bacon, cut into small dice
1 medium onion, finely chopped
Salt and pepper
300ml milk
100ml cream
225g potatoes, peeled and cut
    into small uneven dice
1 bay leaf, very finely shredded
1 tbsp chopped parsley

500ml fish stock (page 49)

Melt the butter in the pan, add the bacon and fry over a medium heat until golden. Add the onion and some seasoning and cook gently until softened.

Add the milk, cream, potatoes, bay leaf and the fish stock, bring to the boil, then simmer for five to 10 minutes until the potatoes are very soft.

Add the smoked haddock with the chopped parsley and check the seasoning. Gently bring to a simmer then turn off the heat and serve.

Notes

When buying smoked haddock it should not be dyed and bright yellow; this has a smoked flavour added to it. Ask for real smoked haddock; if not available use unsmoked fish.

After the potatoes are cooked you can let it cool down and keep it in the fridge for three or four days, then reheat it and add the fish.

Once the fish is in the hot soup it will start to cook, so be careful not to overheat as the fish will be overcooked and will fall apart.

Empty the Fridge Soup

If you are going away for a week or so, don't throw out your vegetables. Make them into a soup to put in the freezer for your return. The last time I did this I had roughly the amount below. We were not going away, we just did not eat much at home that week and I really needed to use up bits and pieces that were hanging around in the fridge. Serves 8–10 people.

500g onions, roughly chopped
500g carrots, roughly chopped
200g celery
400g parsnips
300g sweet potatoes
Salt and pepper
1.75 litres tap water.

Warm a heavy-based large saucepan. Add a good splash of oil followed by the onions, celery, carrots and a good seasoning of salt and pepper. Mix well.

Cook the vegetables for at least five minutes or until they are starting to soften, on a medium to low heat, mixing now and again.

Turn the heat to the lowest setting (use a heat diffuser if needed), cover with a tight-fitting lid and cook for at least 20 minutes. The longer and slower you do this the better the flavour.

Add the water, parsnip and sweet potatoes. Bring to the boil, lower the heat and simmer for about 15 minutes or until the parsnip and potato are really soft.

Taste and add more seasoning if needed. If it looks too thick, add some more water, bring back to the boil and simmer for five minutes.

Whizz the soup until smooth.

Other bits to use up and add to the soup

A couple of slices of bacon, finely chopped and added with the onions, will give extra flavour. Or grill until crisp and add to the soup before serving.
Ends of cheese – chop into cubes and sprinkle into the soup.
Bread – make croûtons.

Fish Soup

This is a filling fish soup, really a meal in itself. We serve it in the café as a starter and main dish. The soup can be made in advance. Serves 4.

Olive oil

1 medium onion, finely chopped

2 cloves garlic, finely chopped

1 celery stick, finely chopped

½ cucumber, finely chopped

1tbsp parsley, stalks and leaves

2 sprigs thyme

½tsp saffron filaments

1 x 400g tin tomatoes,
   chopped, and their juice

½ bottle dry white wine

1 lemon, juiced

Salt and pepper

A selection of very fresh fish

600ml fish stock (page 49)

Heat a large saucepan, add a good splash of oil and sweat the onion and celery for at least 10 minutes. Season well with salt and pepper.

Add the garlic, cucumber, herbs, saffron, tomatoes, stock and wine, bring to the boil and simmer for 15 minutes. Then add a good squeeze of lemon juice, taste and add salt and pepper if needed. (At this stage you can cool the soup down and store in the fridge until needed.)

When ready to eat, bring back to the boil.

Add the prepared fish and remove from the heat – the fish will cook in the heat of the soup.

Taste and adjust seasoning if needed.

Serve.

Short cut

Take tomato sauce and fish stock from the freezer, defrost, mix together and bring to the boil. Add some wine, saffron and lemon juice, simmer for 15 minutes and finish as above.

Posh it up

Add a mixture of fish including mussels, scallops, squid and clams and serve with croûtons, garlic mayonnaise and a spicy red pepper sauce. This works well as a main course.

Turnip and Ginger Soup

Serves 4–6 people.

Olive oil

2 medium onions,
  roughly chopped

2 celery sticks, roughly chopped

1 carrot, chopped

A good thumb-size piece
  root ginger

Salt and pepper

1 litre tap water

400g turnip, peeled and
  chopped

Warm a heavy-based large saucepan, add a good splash of oil followed by the onions, celery, carrot, grated ginger and a good pinch of salt and pepper. Mix well.

Cook the vegetables for at least five minutes or until they are starting to soften, on a medium-to-low heat, mixing now and again.

Turn the heat to the lowest (use a heat diffuser if needed), cover with a tight-fitting lid and cook for at least 20 minutes. The longer and slower you do this the better the flavour.

Add the water and the turnip, bring to the boil and simmer for 20 minutes or until the turnip is very soft.

Taste and add more seasoning if needed. If it looks too thick, add some more water, bring back to the boil and simmer for five minutes.

Whizz the soup until smooth.

Gazpacho

This is really a vegetable smoothy. Over the past few years it has become more popular in the café and the cookery students are always surprised how simple and tasty it is.

1.5kg ripe tomatoes
½ cucumber
½ head garlic
3 spring onions
1 large red pepper
125ml olive oil
45ml vinegar
Salt and pepper
Cayenne (just a pinch)
750ml cold water
A handful of breadcrumbs or
    1 medium carrot, grated

Roughly chop all the vegetables and mix with the olive oil, vinegar, water, breadcrumbs or carrot, salt and pepper, and liquidise or whizz until smooth.
Let it rest in the fridge for a couple of hours.
Serve cold.

To posh it up
Finely chop some spring onion, red pepper, cucumber and fennel. Serve in separate bowls for people to add as they like.

Nettle and Potato Soup

About 500g or about ½ carrier
    bag full of nettle tops or
    young leaves
Olive oil
2 large onions, chopped
2 large carrots, chopped
3 celery sticks, chopped
Salt and pepper
1 litre of tap water
A few gratings of nutmeg
3 medium potatoes, about
    300g, roughly chopped

Pick the leaves off the nettles and wash them thoroughly. Discard only the tougher stalks, as the soup will be whizzed. Heat a medium-sized, heavy-based saucepan. Add a good splash of olive oil and sweat the onions, the carrots and celery until soft but not brown. Season well with salt and pepper. You need to do this for at least five minutes on a medium-to-low heat.

Heat on the lowest setting (use a heat diffuser if needed), cover with a lid and cook for at least 20 minutes. The longer and slower you do this the better the flavour.

Add the water and the potatoes, bring to the boil and simmer for 5–10 minutes, until the potatoes are tender. Season with nutmeg and add the nettles, piling them in, bring back to the boil and simmer for a couple of minutes.

Whizz up. Serve at once or cool down in a big mixing bowl (this will keep its nice green colour) and keep in the fridge until needed.

A little extra

Serve with cream, crème fraîche, or yoghurt topped with toasted rolled oats.

Sweet Things

Sweet Things

In this chapter there are eight very simple but impressive desserts and puddings.

All of these desserts can be made in minutes and all bar the prune clafoutis are flourless. The rice pudding and clafoutis contain dairy produce, otherwise the sweets are dairy-free unless you serve with cream.

The fruit desserts made with a syrup work as a good base and you can change the flavour and fruit depending on what is available and what you have in the kitchen. Once when on holiday we wanted a quick dessert and the only fresh fruit I could find in the local shop was bananas. So I got a tin of pineapple and made a syrup with some fresh ginger and chilli (which were left in the fridge by the previous guests). When it cooled, I mixed in the sliced bananas and served with some ice-cream and hot chocolate sauce.

In the past I used to make a dessert once a week on a Friday evening or for Sunday lunch and use it as a bribe to get my children to try everything during the week. It worked and now I only make a dessert when friends come round!

Do try natural yoghurt with the fruit recipes. It does take a while to like, but this is the best way to introduce it to your diet. One gram of natural yoghurt has 10 million live (good) bacteria which are vital to your digestive well-being.

Bananas in Lime Syrup

*I had this for breakfast every morning, served with yoghurt, while on holiday in Egypt.
Now I have it for dessert with cream and also serve it with hot and spicy curries.
One of the most simple and versatile fruit dishes ever, and you can use up those last
few bananas that are starting to look a little sad in the fruit bowl.*

200g sugar
250ml water
Zest and juice of two limes
4 bananas

Put the sugar, water and lime zest in a saucepan and bring
slowly to the boil, stirring now and again until the sugar
dissolves. Lower the heat and simmer for five minutes.
Leave to cool.
In the meantime, slice the bananas into a bowl.
Pour the lime juice over them.
When the syrup is completely cold, pour it over the bananas
and mix well.

Poires Savoyards

Everybody is amazed how easy this dish is.

4 large pears
Knob unsalted butter
4tbsp caster sugar
175ml double cream
1 vanilla pod, split and the
    seeds scraped out

Preheat the oven to 200°/Gas 6.
Peel the pears, halve, remove the cores and quarter.
Butter a shallow ovenproof dish and arrange the pears in it,
overlapping. Sprinkle on the sugar and pour the cream over it.
Add the vanilla seeds along with the pod and mix in well with
the cream and the pears. Bake for 20 minutes. Let it cool
slightly and serve.

Notes
*You could sprinkle some toasted slivered almonds on the top
just before serving if you have some in the kitchen or try toasted
pinenuts.*

Pears in Vanilla Syrup

4 pears, peeled, cored and
   halved
200g sugar
250ml water
1 vanilla pod, split and scraped

Put the sugar, water and vanilla pods into a saucepan and bring slowly to the boil, stirring until the sugar dissolves. Boil for just two minutes.

Next add the pears and poach until soft – about 15 minutes – and allow to macerate for several hours.

Serve with natural yoghurt or lightly whipped cream.

Notes

Cream is best here.

Toasted pinenuts sprinkled over just before serving are lovely.

In the summer you could use cherries or peaches instead.

Any leftover syrup can be kept in the fridge for at least a week and poured over ice-cream.

St Emilion au Chocolat

Chocolate dessert is a must now and again and I think this is one of the best, especially after a fish main course. We once had a man come on a course just to learn how to make this for his wife!

250g dark chocolate, the best
    you can buy
½ tbsp instant coffee
125ml water
4 large eggs
4 macaroons
A drop of brandy

In a medium-sized saucepan bring the water to the boil and add the coffee. Remove from the heat and add the chocolate broken into pieces. Stir to help it melt.

Separate the eggs, lightly beat the yolks, add to the hot chocolate mixture and mix well until the mixture thickens a little.

In the meantime beat the egg whites until very stiff and fold into the hot chocolate mixture. The egg white will melt into the chocolate as it is hot but this is what makes it so intense. Divide the mixture between eight small cups or ramekins. Lay the macaroons on a plate and soak with the brandy. Stuff one into the middle of each mousse.

Leave to set in the fridge for at least a couple of hours (they will keep for four or five days in the fridge at this stage). Top with some lightly whipped cream and serve.

Notes

Macaroons are flourless and are easy to find. Our local fish shop sells them!

Prune Clafoutis

150ml dark rum,
   plus 1tbsp for serving
150ml water
50g caster or vanilla sugar
200g prunes, ready-soaked
   and stoned
75g plain flour, sieved
50g sugar
3 medium eggs
425ml milk
25g unsalted butter, plus extra
   for greasing the dish
Icing sugar, for dusting

Preheat the oven to 200°/Gas 7. Make the batter by mixing the flour and sugar together in a large bowl. In another bowl beat the eggs and add the milk. Now slowly add to the flour mixture as you whisk it all together, or put everything in a blender until smooth and leave to rest while the prunes are cooking.

For the prunes, place the rum, the water and sugar in a small saucepan and bring to the boil. Add the prunes and simmer for 15–25 minutes until all the liquid has been absorbed and the prunes are coated in a sticky syrup.

Butter a 35cm oval gratin dish (or other shallow ovenproof dish of equivalent dimensions). Re-whisk the batter if necessary and then pour it into the dish. Scatter the prunes and syrup evenly over the surface. Dot with the butter and bake for 25–30 minutes. When it comes out of the oven it will be impressively puffed and golden, sinking after a few minutes. Sprinkle over the remaining tablespoon of rum and serve.

Rice Pudding

The best rice pudding. Lovely hot or cold.

50g butter
75g sugar
100g round grain pudding rice
1 litre of full-cream milk
150ml cream
Tiny pinch of salt

1 medium flameproof pot or dish (I usually use a cast iron saucepan; just make sure there is no plastic or wood attached)

Preheat the oven to 140°/Gas 1.

Melt the butter in an ovenproof saucepan and add the sugar. Stir and continue to cook until it looks like toffee.

Add the rice and continue stirring for 2–3 minutes. Pour in the milk, cream and salt and mix well. Bring to the boil, stirring every few minutes to help the sugar dissolve.

Place in the oven and leave to cook for 2–2½ hours – or until just beginning to set.

Leave to cool for at least 15 minutes before serving.

Notes
Pudding rice is the same as risotto rice.

Hot Chocolate and Orange Sauce

*Just the sauce to turn some good shop-bought ice-cream into a great dessert.
I have this sauce on my list of food bribes and it always works. I use it mostly when
I am encouraging my daughter to eat up her fish.*

175g bitter chocolate,
     broken into pieces
Juice and zest of 1 orange
25g sugar
25g butter, soft
2 egg yolks, lightly beaten

Place chocolate pieces with the juice and zest of the orange,
the sugar, the butter and two tablespoons of water in a
saucepan and stir over a low heat as the chocolate melts.
Once it is all happily amalgamated, leave it to get thoroughly
hot, without actually boiling.
Remove from the heat and beat in the egg yolks.
Serve at once poured over vanilla ice-cream.

Raspberries with Lemon-scented Geranium Leaves or Lemon Grass

500g frozen raspberries
200g sugar
225ml water
4 large geranium leaves or
  1 stick of lemon grass cut
  into 4

Put the berries in a bowl.

Put the sugar, water and geranium leaves or lemon grass into a saucepan and bring slowly to the boil, stirring until the sugar dissolves. Boil for just two minutes.

Cool for four or five minutes, then pour the hot syrup over the fruit and allow to macerate for several hours.

Remove the leaves or lemon grass and serve chilled with cream or ice-cream.

A Few More
Good Things

A Few More Good Things

This chapter is an assortment of recipes that people have asked me for over the years that I could not fit into the weekly chapters. They vary from something as simple as hummus to a roast rib of beef and also a very simple porter cake.

I have included my spinach and Durrus cheese pizza, which we have served at the café for lunch since opening in 2003. Many people have asked us for this recipe. Now you can make it at home and you will not need a special pizza oven, just a very hot metal tray.

Baked Sweet Potatoes with Chilli and Lime Butter

Sometimes we need something a bit different.

4 large sweet potatoes
A medium-sized red chilli
   pepper or a dried chilli
   soaked in boiling water for
   5 minutes
Juice of a lime
100g butter, very soft
A small handful of coriander
   leaves

Heat the oven to its hottest; this should take about 10 to 15 minutes.

Sweet potatoes tend to leak a sugary juice when they are baked, so put a tray on the bottom of the oven to catch the juices and bake the potatoes on the oven rack for about an hour.

Meanwhile, chop the chilli finely.

Put the chopped chilli, lime juice and butter together in a bowl and mix well with your hands.

Split the cooked potato in half, stuff with the chilli butter and eat while hot.

Notes

Try this with the lentil salad instead of a regular potato.
If the chilli is too hot for you, remove the seeds.

Beef and Carrots

I had to put this recipe in. It was one of the first dishes I had with the de Montault family in France when I was an au pair for them. Twenty-five years ago when I had this dish along with many other simple dishes, I was amazed how good it was with so few ingredients and very little effort. I returned the following summer to learn more.
I gave this recipe to Jane Grigson, who put it in her book English Food.
This is another dish that benefits from being cooked the day before.

2–2.5kg rolled brisket of beef
Olive oil
6–8 firm large carrots, peeled
1 litre chicken stock
Generous sprig of thyme
Salt, pepper and parsley

Serve with boiled potatoes

Take a heavy-based saucepan that will fit the meat closely. Heat the saucepan and add a splash of oil, enough to coat the bottom of the pan.

Season the beef with salt and pepper and brown on all sides. Slice the carrots thinly, in the processor or with a slicer, and pile half of them around the beef. Pour in stock to come 5–7cm up the pot and tuck in the thyme. Bring to the boil. Reduce heat and simmer for five minutes. Pile in the rest of the carrots, push down around and on top of the meat and cover. The lid need not fit very tightly, as a certain amount of evaporation is desirable.

Keep the pot at a gentle bubble, checking it every half hour or so, topping up the liquid level with more stock and giving the carrots a good mix. After two hours it should be cooked, but be prepared to give it a further half hour if not.

Transfer the beef to a hot serving dish and surround with the drained carrots, which will be extremely succulent. Season them, sprinkle with parsley and keep warm. Strain the cooking liquid into a shallow pan and boil down to concentrate the flavour. Season and pour a little over the beef and carrots and the rest into a hot sauceboat. Boiled potatoes go well with this dish.

Notes
Topside would work well here. It's just a little more expensive and I like a little fat for flavour.

Beetroot with Yoghurt

Here is another recipe for beetroot. This does not resemble the beetroot pickled in jars which we grew up with. Blank that memory from your mind and give this a try.

500g beetroot
A squeeze of lemon
1 tbsp olive oil
1 small bunch fresh flat-leaf
    parsley leaves, roughly
    chopped
Salt and pepper

To serve
1 garlic clove, crushed
200g natural yoghurt
Olive oil
1 tsp nigella seeds or
    onion seeds
Salt

Wash the beetroot carefully without piercing the skin, otherwise they will bleed.

Place in a saucepan of cold salted water and bring to the boil. Depending on the size of the beetroot, this will take anywhere from half an hour to an hour. They will be ready when you can slip a sharp knife easily into the centre, rather like testing to see if a potato is cooked. (If your oven is already on and being used to cook another dish, wrap the beetroot in foil and bake until done.)

Drain and rub away the skin with your fingers. If the beetroot is cooked, the skin should come away very easily.

Cut into 1cm rounds, arrange on a plate and dress with the lemon juice, olive oil, parsley, salt and pepper.

Mix the garlic with the yoghurt and check for seasoning.

Pour over the beetroot, drizzle with a little olive oil and sprinkle on the nigella seeds.

We also serve this dish warm, as it is delicious with grilled fish or chicken. The beetroot bleeds into the yoghurt, turning the sauce bright purple.

Planning ahead
I find roasting the beetroot gives it a better flavour.

Brisket of Beef with Onions and Soy

An interesting recipe for a very under-used cut of meat. We served it in the café one summer and many customers wanted the recipe.

2.5kg brisket of beef on the bone
250ml honey, mild flavour
6 big thumbs fresh ginger,
    peeled and grated
A little salt and lots of black
    pepper
6 cloves of garlic, peeled and
    chopped
2 medium onions, peeled and
    sliced
200ml soy sauce or tamari
400ml boiling water

Serve with roasted turnip with
ginger

Take the meat and make as many incisions as you can so the marinade will make an impact.

Combine honey, ginger, garlic, salt and pepper in a bowl and rub all over the beef, making sure it gets into the slits you have made. Cover tightly with clingfilm or put into a plastic bag and tie up and refrigerate for 4–12 hours, tossing once or twice to make sure it marinates evenly.

Preheat the oven to 200°/Gas 5.

Place the brisket and marinade into a roasting tray on top of the onions, making sure you put it meat-side down (bone facing up) on the tray. Add soy and water and cover tightly with tin foil.

Bake for three hours, then remove the cover and turn the beef over, meat-side up.

Cook for a further hour, basting with the cooking juices, until the meat is dark brown and caramelised and is beginning to come off the bones.

Roasted Turnips with Ginger

½ medium turnip
2cm thumb of fresh ginger
Olive oil
Salt and pepper

Heat the oven to its hottest temperature and warm a flat roasting tray.

Peel and cut the turnip into 1cm cubes.

Peel and grate the ginger.

Put the turnip along with the ginger, salt and pepper and enough oil to lightly coat the vegetable into a mixing bowl and mix well.

Spread the turnip evenly on the tray and roast for about 30 to 40 minutes or until soft right through and slightly charred at the edges.

Cashel Blue Cheese, Pear and Spinach on Toast

Heat the grill while you toast a thick slice of bread on both sides. Pile on some baby spinach, rocket or watercress followed by half a sliced pear and topped with a generous slice of Cashel blue cheese.

Pop under the grill for a couple of minutes or until the cheese is nicely melted and starting to bubble.

Notes

A great lunch dish or ideal as a starter for dinner.
An ideal way to use up the ends of blue cheese left after Christmas.

Durrus Cheese, Spinach and Nutmeg Pizza

This is our most popular lunch dish at Good Things and the idea came about when all I had was a bag of spinach and an old Durrus cheese. Makes two large pizzas, enough for four people.

1 recipe of pizza dough (if you manage to roll the dough very thin, you will have extra for another day)

4–5 large handfuls of roughly chopped spinach, stalks removed

Salt, pepper and lots of freshly grated nutmeg

12 thin slices Durrus cheese (about 200g) with rind removed

Olive oil

Handful of fine brown flour for rolling

Heat the oven to its hottest temperature and heat two flat baking trays with no sides. This is essential for a crispy base. Divide the pizza dough in half and roll each piece very thinly, using the fine flour to dust the worktop.

Place on the hot baking tray and top with the spinach.

Season with salt, pepper and grated nutmeg.

Arrange the slices of cheese on top.

Drizzle with olive oil and bake in the hot oven for 8 to 10 minutes until the base is golden and crispy and the cheese has melted.

Notes

Instead of spinach you can use Swiss chard, beetroot tops or seabeet.

If you cannot get Durrus cheese, use a strong semi-soft cheese, preferably unpasteurised, as the flavour is better for cooking.

Collar of Ham with Apple Juice and Juniper

1–2kg collar of ham
2 leeks, roughly chopped
1 carrot, roughly chopped
2 celery sticks, roughly
  chopped
15 juniper berries
1 cinnamon stick
6 black peppercorns
A few parsley stalks
2 bay leaves
1 litre of apple juice

First, bring the ham to the boil in a saucepan of water, then drain and rinse it under the tap

Put the ham back into the saucepan and pour in the apple juice along with all the other ingredients.

Add enough water to cover the ham.

Bring the pot to the boil, turn the heat down, simmer and scoop off any foam that comes to the top.

Leave to cook for one and a half to two hours, depending on the thickness. Turn off the heat and leave the ham in the cooking liquid for 20 minutes before serving.

Cut the ham into thick slices. Serve with a jug of the poaching liquid, mashed potatoes and a salad of cabbage, apple and toasted pumpkin seeds (page 303).

Cabbage, Apple and Toasted Pumpkin Seed Salad

I made this salad one day when I had a little cabbage left in the fridge. There was not enough to cook, so I decided to make it into a salad with some apples and toasted seeds.

About 125–150g cabbage
  (Savoy is the best here),
  thinly sliced
1 red onion, thinly sliced
1 carrot, grated
2 apples, cored and thinly sliced
Olive oil
Cider vinegar
½ tsp mixed spice
20g pumpkin seeds

Mix all the vegetables and apples together.
Add the mixed spice, salt, pepper and cider vinegar to taste.
Mix in a good splash of oil and leave to stand for a few minutes.
In the meantime, toast the pumpkin seeds in a dry pan and add while hot to the salad. Mix in well.
Serve at once. So good!

Hummus

150g dried chickpeas
   (or 1 tin)
Juice of 2 lemons
4 cloves of garlic
100g tahini
Cumin seeds, to taste
Cayenne pepper, to taste
Salt
Olive oil

Cook the chickpeas, drain them and save the liquid.
Put about four tablespoons of the cooking liquid into the blender and add the lemon juice and garlic. Turn the blender to high, add the chickpeas and the tahini and blend well. If the mixture clogs, add a little more liquid and some olive oil. You need to end up with a thick, creamy purée.
Season with cumin seeds, a pinch of cayenne pepper and salt. Serve with a salsa made with a little onion, cucumber, red pepper and tomato, seasoned and finished off with lemon juice and olive oil.

Notes

Make extra and keep in the fridge, as it goes really well with grilled or roast lamb. Also lovely inside grilled aubergines, sprinkled with chopped coriander and rolled up.

Omelette Arnold Bennett

Great for breakfast, lunch or dinner. Fast, easy and so good to eat, just make sure you can get the undyed smoked haddock. Serves 2 people.

6 eggs

salt and pepper

100g smoked haddock
    (uncooked)

60g grated Parmesan cheese

1tbsp cream

A good knob of butter

23cm crêpe or omelette pan

Heat your grill.

Beat the eggs in a bowl and season with salt and pepper.

Heat your pan and add the butter. Brown the butter until golden then add your beaten eggs and continue to beat in the pan for a few seconds.

Remove from the heat before it sets (you just want it a little runny).

Add the smoked haddock, cheese and cream and put under the grill.

The omelette is done when the fish is cooked and the eggs are puffy.

Oxtail with Wholegrain Mustard

I had to include this recipe as it is so simple with amazing results. Don't be put off by the tail; you are in for a real treat. This is another dish that improves when cooked at least a day in advance. Don't forget to pick up the bones and have a good chew!

Olive oil
2 oxtails, chopped
Salt and pepper
2–3 large onions, sliced
3 bay leaves
200ml white wine
2tbsp wholegrain
   mustard
400ml double cream

Preheat the oven to 150°/Gas 2.

Heat a shallow pan with a lid and in the meantime season the oxtail well with salt and pepper.

When the pan is very hot, add a good splash of olive oil and start browning the oxtail. You will have to do this in about three batches, transferring the meat to a plate as you go.

Add another drop of oil to the pan and soften the onions for a few minutes, as they clean the pan.

Place the oxtail on top of the onions, add the bay leaves and pour in the wine.

Bring to the boil and let simmer for a minute.

Cover with a disc of greaseproof paper followed by the lid.

Cook in the oven for at least two hours, maybe three, or until the meat is leaving the bone.

Remove from the oven. Transfer the oxtail to a plate.

Place the pot on a medium flame and add the mustard and cream.

Mix well and let simmer for four or five minutes. Return the oxtail to the pan, coat well in the mustardy cream sauce and simmer for a further five minutes.

Serve with mashed or boiled potatoes.

Notes

If making in advance – remove from the oven, cool down and keep in the fridge. When needed, bring the cream and mustard to the boil, add to the oxtail, simmer for 15 minutes on a low heat and serve.

307

Piedmontese Peppers

Olive oil
4 red peppers
4 garlic cloves, sliced thinly
20 cherry tomatoes, halved, or
    8 tomatoes, halved
16 tinned salted anchovies

Preheat the oven to 220°/Gas 7.

Split the peppers in half lengthways and remove the core, white pith and seeds.

Oil an ovenproof dish or pan and sit the peppers snugly into it. Season with salt and pepper and fill with the garlic, tomatoes and anchovies. Sprinkle well with olive oil.

Roast in the oven for 45 minutes or until the peppers are starting to char at the edges and the tomatoes have totally softened.

Serve with bread to mop up the juices.

Roast Rib of Beef

3kg rib of beef on the bone

Gravy (page 34)

Set your oven to its hottest temperature and prepare your roasting tray as for any of the roasting recipes. For beef I like to use mainly onions for my vegetable bed and then use some of them in the gravy. Rub the joint all over with a little olive oil and season really well with salt, pepper and a teaspoon of powdered mustard.

Place in the very hot oven and roast for 30 minutes or until the fat is nice and brown and starting to crisp.

Turn the heat down to 200°/Gas 6 and cook for another hour for rare beef, adding another 15 minutes for medium and another 30 for well done. Remove from the oven.

Transfer the meat to a plate and keep in a warm place for 30 minutes while you make the gravy and finish everything off. Serve with roast potatoes, a tray of roast parsnips and horseradish sauce.

Horseradish, Crème Fraîche and Mustard Sauce

This just adds that something special to your roast beef.

3tbsp creamed horseradish
    sauce
1tbsp crème fraîche
2tbsp wholegrain mustard
Salt and pepper

Mix all the ingredients together at least 15 minutes before you are going to eat, or make it the day before if you can.

Ragoût of Duck Wings

This recipe evolved in the café during the summer of 2008 as a result of the lack of sunny days. I decided we needed a comfort dish to appeal to customers feeling a bit washed out by our unpredictable Irish weather. We had lots of duck wings, nice streaky bacon and a selection of spices. The waiting staff were rather dubious – a stew of duck wings! Darina Allen from Ballymaloe was booked in for lunch that day and I knew this was her kind of dish. So the kitchen versus front-of-house bet was laid and we sold six portions that day, with many requests for the recipe. It became our most popular lunch dish after the Durrus cheese pizza.

Always try and have some duck or chicken stock in the freezer, as it is really the ingredient that gives this stew its rich flavour and makes this dish seem uncomplicated.

12 duck wings

Salt and pepper

Olive oil

2 large onions, finely chopped

2 celery sticks, finely chopped

50g cubed streaky bacon

400ml chicken or duck stock

2 tomatoes, roughly chopped

4 large cloves of garlic

1 dried red hot chilli, finely
  chopped

½ tsp ground gloves

A good grating of nutmeg

1 cinnamon stick

While you warm a heavy-based saucepan, dry the wings with kitchen paper, put them into a large bowl and season with salt and pepper. When the pan is warm add a little olive oil and cook the bacon until the fat softens. Remove and add the wings. Brown the wings on both sides – you might need to do this in two batches. Remove from the pot.

Add the onions and celery and cook on a medium heat until they start to soften. Return the bacon and wings to the pot and add the stock, bring to the boil and add the tomatoes, garlic, chilli and spices. Reduce the heat to just a tiny bubble and cook for an hour and a half or until the meat is starting to fall off the bone.

Keep warm in the saucepan while you reduce some of the sauce. Pour about half of the sauce into a shallow saucepan or a deep frying pan, put it on a high heat and boil for at least 10 minutes to reduce and improve the flavour.

Pour the sauce over the the wings and serve from the pot with a big bowl of pasta.

Porter Cake

I am including this recipe as it is the most sought-after recipe at the café and cookery class. We always have one on the go for the students to pick at during the week. One student emailed me last week to say she made it in the morning, had some friends around in the evening and the cake was eaten. I was given this recipe by Mary Keane of Keane's bar in the Maam valley in Co. Galway years ago. I have made many of them since and we serve them in the café. I also make them for weddings. The recipe is so easy you cannot go wrong.

500g plain flour

1tsp mixed spice

250g butter

250g soft brown sugar

1 level teaspoon of bread soda

4 eggs, lightly beaten

500g currants

500g sultanas

250ml bottle of stout
  (dark beer)

In a large saucepan mix together the mixed spice, butter and sugar and add half of the stout.

Heat the mixture gently and let it simmer lightly until everything has melted. Next add the fruit.

Mix the rest of the stout with the bread soda and combine with the beaten eggs, then add to the mixture in the saucepan and finally fold in the flour.

Bake in a lined 25cm round tin at 150°/Gas 3–4.

Bake for about two hours until a knife pushed into the centre comes out clean.

Do check from time to time in case the top is burning; if so turn the oven down to suit.

Notes

No margarine, use only butter.

Buy the best fruit you can. A good health food shop is the place to go.

I use unrefined sugar, as it is less sweet.

This cake freezes well and will keep in a cake tin for 1–2 weeks.

Lovely with a litte butter or, as they do in the north of England, with some nice Cheddar cheese.

Apple and Blackberry Crumble

I had to add this crumble recipe as it is so good. I like the way it uses linseeds, and the cider custard is not to be missed.

500g apples, cored and
    chopped into small chunks
500g blackberries or 1kg
    cooking apples when the
    blackberries are gone

For the crumble

175g self-raising flour
75g cold butter
110g dark brown sugar
100g linseeds
A handful of rolled oats

Preheat the oven to 180°/Gas 5.

Put the apples and blackberries in a large baking dish.

Put the flour into a large mixing bowl, grate the butter (on the coarse side of a square grater) into the flour and finish by rubbing it in with your fingers until it looks like coarse sand, then mix in the sugar. Mix in the linseeds to make it crunchy, then spoon the crumble mix over the fruit in the baking dish, compacting it fairly firmly.

Sprinkle the oats on top and bake for 40 minutes.

Notes

Substitute other fruit if you like. Rhubarb is very good.

Cider Custard

2 egg yolks
200ml good dry cider or a
    good pressed apple juice
2tbsp muscovado sugar
1tbsp cornflour or potato flour
½tsp cinnamon
400ml cream

In a saucepan over a low heat, mix together the first five ingredients with a whisk until well combined.

Add the cream, whisking constantly, and continue to whisk until the custard has thickened, not letting it boil.

Taste and if you want a more creamy custard add a drop more cream.

Chocolate and Banana Cake

So easy, and a big hit in the café. We serve it warm with some cookies-and-cream ice-cream. We make this in our practical cookery classes. People who have never made a cake before are delighted with the result and it becomes a family favourite. It has been referred to as the "feck it in cake" by many a male student! Double the recipe to make a birthday cake or make two cakes and freeze one. For a quick fix, make into muffins. Best of all, you get to use up those black bananas.

170g butter, softened
170g sugar
135g dark chocolate
280g self-raising flour
Pinch of salt
½tsp bread soda
3 large eggs
2 bananas (the black ones at the bottom of the fruit bowl that nobody wants to eat!)

Preheat the oven to 160°/Gas 5.

Place the butter in a saucepan and set over a low heat until the butter has melted. Add the sugar, giving it the odd stir.

Turn off the heat, add the chocolate and melt that too.

Mix the flour, salt and bread soda together; put the soda through a sieve to avoid lumps.

Beat the eggs and mash the bananas with a fork.

Finally mix everything together in the saucepan, folding in well.

Turn into a buttered or lined 1kg loaf tin.

Bake in the oven for about 45 minutes.

Do check the cake after about 35 minutes. You want it a little moist in the centre, but not sticky.

Index